# SUSTAINABLE SMALL SCHOOLS

# SUSTAINABLE SMALL SCHOOLS:
# A HANDBOOK FOR RURAL COMMUNITIES

Edited by
Craig B. Howley
and
John M. Eckman

# WITHDRAWN

Clearinghouse on Rural Education and Small Schools
Charleston, West Virginia

**ERIC**®

Clearinghouse on Rural Education and Small Schools
Appalachia Educational Laboratory
P.O. Box 1348, Charleston, WV 25325

Illustrations by John Macdonald, Williamstown, MA
Cover design by Rich Hendel, Chapel Hill, NC

**Library of Congress Cataloging-in-Publication Data**


Howley, Craig B.
Sustainable small schools : a handbook for rural communities / edited by
Craig B. Howley and John M. Eckman.
p. cm.
Includes bibliographical references and index.
ISBN 1-880785-16-1
1. Rural schools—United States—Handbooks, manuals, etc.
2. Education, Rural—United States—Handbooks, manuals, etc.
I. Howley, Craig B.          II. Eckman, John M., 1959-
LC5146.5.S87 1997
370.19'346'0973—DC20                                    96-33073
                                                            CIP

The Mountain Institute is a private, non-profit organization dedicated to advancing mountain cultures and preserving mountain environments. From its international headquarters in Franklin, West Virginia, The Mountain Institute conducts conservation, development, and education programs in the Andes, Appalachian, and Himalayan ranges. More information regarding the Institute and its work is available by calling 304.358.2401 or by visiting www.mountain.org on the world wide web.

This publication was prepared with funding from the U. S. Department of Education, Office of Educational Research and Improvement, under Contract No. RR93002012. The opinions expressed herein do not necessarily reflect the positions or policies of the Office of Educational Research and Improvement or the Department of Education.
The ERIC Clearinghouse on Rural Education and Small Schools is operated by the Appalachia Educational Laboratory (AEL), Inc. AEL is an Affirmative Action/Equal Opportunity Employer.

# Table of Contents

# Preface

This book is for you—parents, concerned citizens, and educators—and for your children, your school, and your community. We offer it to help you find resources, design school options, and take action together. We have tried to make this book especially useful and accessible to people who are *not* educators, but we fully imagine that educators will be able to use it also. Our treatment is not academic or "scholarly." But all of the ideas and information are based on professional thinking and studies, and there are plenty of clear pointers to the professional literature (see chapter 6 for resources and chapter 2 for an extended bibliography).

The communities of which rural schools are a part differ dramatically from each other. This means that the people who use this handbook will read it with very different perspectives. We hope reading this book will help you realize your own powers for creating options and be useful as you put that knowledge into action.

## How to Use this Book

The book is organized into five chapters plus an extended resource chapter that points you to other readings, organizations, and people. The chapters are described next, but you can really start reading anywhere; you can even read this book backwards. For example, *if you are most concerned about—*

- who makes decisions and how to work with them—start with chapter 5;

- organizing or administering small rural schools—start with chapter 4;

- curriculum for small rural schools—start with chapter 3;

- ideas and facts about small schools and consolidation—start with chapter 2;

- where to start and why (what's the big deal?)—start with chapter 1.

Here's what you'll find in the various chapters and resource sections:

## Chapter 1. Your School and Community: Small on Purpose
Basic assumptions; rural schools are small (and what this means); habits of involvement; the power to change; making miracles.

## Chapter 2. Healthy Rural Schools, Good Rural Schools
Some major ideas about mass schooling—aims, history, and industrial society; information about consolidation and small schools; information about state policy making; a bibliography of sources.

### Chapter 3. What Others Have Done: Community as Focus of Study

Examples of various rural programs and activities in which the community inspires the curriculum. (As you read, keep the ideas in mind, and remember that programs are not magic bullets; every time a program is adapted it is re-created.)

### Chapter 4. What Others Have Done: Options for Keeping School

Examples of various programs and tactics for organizing rural schools, including the 4-day week, the multigrade classroom, electronic technology. (Again, the focus is not on things or programs, but ideas.)

### Chapter 5. Doing it Yourself: Helping Things to Change

Developing ideas for change is one thing, helping things change is another; strategic and tactical tips for making change happen.

### Chapter 6. Resources

Organized into eight sections: partnerships; coalition building; needs assessment; consolidation; featured options (e.g., Foxfire, the 4-day week); rural resources from regional educational laboratories; tools for finding information; and rural education organizations.

So look through the entire book. Read in more detail the sections that relate directly to your concerns. Do something, even if it's only to start a conversation. Breaking the silence helps us all realize a change for the better. —CBH

# Acknowledgments

This handbook has been six years in the making, a process that started like a small stream up in the hills and grew as new information and the fresh energies of others added to its flow. It began as the work of people in a small West Virginia town whose personal and professional concern for their rural schools was shared by other parents and educators. As the ideas for the book grew and the scope of the subject became clear, we sought out and found expertise and input from across the country. The final product you hold is the work of many hands and voices, but only a few can be thanked here.

This book evolved out of the Community Schools Program of The Mountain Institute in 1990 and 1991 under the thoughtful and inspired direction of Jennifer Taylor-Ide with Daniel Taylor-Ide and John Villaume assisting in the original drafting. We owe a great debt to the members of the Community Schools Advisory Group, who assembled in West Virginia to consider the issues of rural community schools, their future and the potential impacts of parents and concerned citizens in helping schools find their place in communities. Thanks to advisors Alan DeYoung, Mercedes Fitzmaurice, Ben Guido, Daniel Mastrobuono, Paul Nachtigal, Jacqueline Spears, Robert Stephens, Todd Strohmenger, and Rachel Tompkins. Their wisdom and guidance, from that original meeting to this day, has been an inspiration to this work.

Helping these ideas find rich soil for growth were the John R. McCune Charitable Trust and the Geraldine R. Dodge Foundation, whose generous financial support initiated the research and supported the original program and drafting.

Finally, we would like to thank AEL, Inc., the host institution of the ERIC Clearinghouse on Rural Education and Small Schools, particularly AEL's Rural Center, which provided support for development at a critical juncture. Rural Center staff were particularly helpful in developing the handbook's resource chapter: Phyllis Stowers, Pat Penn, Hobart Harmon, and Carol Perroncel. The revised manuscript was reviewed by members of the Clearinghouse Editorial Board, as well as by staff of The Mountain Institute and the Appalachia Educational Laboratory. Pat Penn, of the Rural Center, provided expert copyediting of the first revised draft. Following external review, Pat Hammer, managing editor of the Clearinghouse, copyedited the final draft. Carla McClure and Kim Cowley of AEL proofread the manuscript and Velma Mitchell, secretary at the Clearinghouse, entered the innumerable changes and proofread the manuscript once again. Marsha Pritt provided typesetting and layout assistance.

This handbook results from the extended collaboration of many individuals and organizations. We hope that it will foster other collaborations, collaborations that strengthen small schools, particularly in rural places. With many others, we believe that America needs more small schools. For that reason, we hope that some of those who find their way here will discover the will to establish *new* small schools. What an innovation that would be in rural communities!

John Eckman
  The Mountain Institute
Craig Howley
  ERIC Clearinghouse on Rural Education and Small Schools and
  the Rural Center at Appalachia Educational Laboratory, Inc.

CHAPTER 1

# Your School and Community: Small on Purpose

R ural schools and communities may differ from one another in significant ways. Some are comparatively affluent, others impoverished. Some have diverse economies; many rely on a single activity (farming, ranching, manufacturing, government lands). In some, the school district is the biggest employer. Some rural communities are mostly American Indian or African American.

But *many* rural schools and *all* rural communities have one thing in common: They are small. Rural people generally appreciate the familiarity of place, land, and kin associated with sparse population or small towns. Maintaining good rural schools and communities means recognizing that being small can be a virtue and needs to be cultivated as such. Unfortunately, such recognition is still not widespread. Cities have been the model of the good life; and while cities can be good places to live, it doesn't necessarily follow that cities should be the model for how to live (or run schools) in rural places. Another way of understanding this situation is to conclude that rural schools and places are *small on purpose*.

If this is the case, people who care about rural schools and communities need to understand the virtues of smallness, and they need to cultivate the purposes peculiar to rural places. Keeping your rural community vital—or perhaps restoring its vitality—will require good local schools. That is the purpose of this book—to help you understand the dilemmas facing your school in the context of rural education as a whole in the United States, and to help you locate resources you need to organize an effort to improve and sustain your small school.

**The power for change.** The most important resource for making good rural schools is the power that you have in combination with friends and neighbors. Part of realizing this power is knowing how to fashion options together and where to go in order to access what you don't have. Most of what your community needs to construct excellent educational experiences is nearer at hand than you may suspect. That's because education is essentially about raising children to become the kind of adults we would like to know and work with.

The basic point is that you don't have to tackle every problem at once. Pick a strand and begin to follow it. Stick with it. Nurture your school. Nurture your involvement and bring other people into the loop. Sustain one another. Share ideas. It will be difficult. But there is no substitute for such dedication. Money certainly can't buy it.

In many cases, getting what you don't have is not very expensive. As the "FAST" science curriculum of the National Diffusion Network demonstrates, you can even have excellent science instruction with minimal equipment (see *Educational Programs That Work*).[1] The Foxfire experience in rural Georgia and elsewhere demonstrates that rural teachers possess incredible reserves of creativity, talent, and commitment.[2] There are also tips for raising supplemental funds and for managing budgets well under existing constraints.

What really matters in schools is what goes on inside. How buildings look, how many degrees teachers have, and the presence of fancy equipment are not important in themselves—such things are symbols, and sometimes they can be symbols for the wrong things.

When you begin to work with the ideas in this book, you will find that they interact and mesh with each other. Let's say that the most pressing problem you face is financial. Chapter 4 discusses the 4-day school week as an alternative schedule. Actually moving to a 4-day week could— through longer class sessions—provide opportunities for more active learning, as considered in Chapter 2. And, because school staff members work on the fifth day, such ventures as planning, decision making, teacher

---

[1] Although the National Diffusion Network has been dismantled, program descriptions are still available in *Educational Programs That Work, The Catalogue of the National Diffusion Network (NDN). 21st Edition*, edited by Gay Lang, available in libraries, the ERIC database, or by ordering from Sopris West, 1140 Boston Ave., Longmont, CO 80501 ($14.95, plus $3.50 handling and shipping for first copy, $1.50 each additional copy).

[2] See chapter 3, p. 48 and *The Active Learner: A Foxfire Journal for Teachers*, described in chapter 6, p. 122.

in-service training, and community involvement (see Chapters 3 and 5) can become feasible and successful.

To be effectively involved takes time, courage, knowledge, organization, persistence, and patience! What you don't have of these, you can develop over time. The work you do will benefit not only the particular children you most care about, but also your community and the wider society of which all our communities are a part.

## Basic Assumptions Underlying this Book

Even though we want this to be a book for everyone, not everyone will agree with the assumptions that have guided its creation. For the record, here they are:

• Everyone has a stake in a community's schools. Parents want their children to be well prepared for life. Community members want young people to grow into responsible neighbors capable of contributing to the community. Educators want to share knowledge and do it well.

• Everyone has a rightful place in making decisions about schooling and education. Schooling is one of the largest undertakings of our government (often the largest single venture at the state level), and our government is founded on the principle of citizen participation. Public education is paid for by the taxes everyone pays. What happens in schools affects society as a whole.

• Good education requires a variety of teaching methods and styles. No one style or method can be best for everyone: Children differ, communities differ, the world changes. The sorts of jobs students face and the kinds of work done in them, for example, have undergone radical changes within a generation.

• Really good learning, true learning, and lasting learning requires teaching that engages students. Call it "active learning" or "hands-on activities" or "authentic instruction"—whatever you call it, it should grab students' imaginations and develop their minds. If this sort of learning happens routinely in a school, the school is wildly successful. In fact, this situation is probably pretty rare.

• Schools and communities are part of one another; they should be seen as such. Closing a school is like removing an essential organ from a community: There had better be a pretty good reason behind such an action. This means that the more schools and communities recognize, celebrate, and develop their inherent connection, the better off they will be.

These may sound like pretty tame assumptions—but each of them has faced strong challenges at times. There is, in fact, a lot of healthy debate about what the purpose of education is, what schools should do, and how schools should be run.

If you are a parent or citizen, you cannot wait for an invitation to participate in school reform. And if you are an educator, you cannot just wait for parents and community members to show up. In the past century, the number of districts fell by 90 percent, and the number of schools fell by more than 50 percent. During this same period, schools became increasingly distant (geographically and philosophically) from parents and community members in many places. After a century of separation, public schools confront great difficulties in reinvolving their communities. Meaningful participation is possible only if educators and citizens each take responsibility for getting together and developing more productive relationships. The most fundamental assumption, then, is this one: Ordinary people from the community need to be involved in public schooling. That involvement is part of what makes public schools *public*.

## Rural and Small—When Less is More

Rural communities and their schools are closely linked in ways that urban and suburban schools cannot be. The local school system is one of the largest employers in a small community; it may even be one of the largest landholders in a small town. Through its payroll, schedule, politics, and students, the school system affects virtually every family in the community, regardless of whether they have children attending school. Whether or not the school makes the most of its local purchasing power, it still plays a major role in a small economy simply by providing the money that many families live on.

On the other hand, the school is heavily influenced by the community. Its budget is affected by local economic conditions. Its students are affected by a rising or falling population base and by the kinds of work available for families in the community. Its educational aspirations and abilities are affected by the human resources and the values of the community. Thus, your community schools both affect and reflect your community's economy. They both affect and reflect your community's politics and values. In short, they affect your community's future in every respect.

Rural communities face difficult times. Rural areas suffer from declining economies, declining populations, decreasing tax bases, increasing costs of services, and a high percentage of fixed-income residents. Rural schools participate in these problems. They face falling enrollments and lower tax support for their services, even as state and federal requirements placed on schools are increasing. Some communities face increases in enrollment that they can't keep up with, while most face school closures and redistricting due to declining enrollment. They may face citizen apathy when many members of the community do not have school-age children.

Furthermore, while schools in general have been severely criticized in recent years, rural people have felt for a very long time that their schools receive *more* than their fair share of such criticism. Small rural schools are often compared unfavorably to their larger urban counterparts. Rural citizens hear, again and again, that their schools are too small to offer the range of courses students need to succeed today, that their teachers aren't qualified to teach the more specialized courses, or that their facilities aren't sufficiently up to date. In many instances, because of such criticisms, rural communities are encouraged to merge their local schools into larger ones serving a larger population base, with the expectation that this will improve the education provided for their children.

Your local school is now required to do more with less, including

- produce higher test scores,

- offer a greater variety of advanced courses,

- introduce modern technology,

- improve facilities, and

- produce graduates with enhanced "employability."

But, in many places, there is also great pressure to

- cut administrative overhead,

- reduce faculty,

- increase class size, and

- hold down taxes.

Some combinations of these requirements are not possible, of course. But there are combinations that will work, provided people get together and make decisions about priorities, commitments, and strategies for action.

Theodore Sizer, a major figure in national school reform, insists that "less is more." He means that schools should focus their curriculum and decide what's important. Not surprisingly, Sizer is convinced that small school size (especially small high schools) helps foster better teaching and learning.

Sizer's slogan ("less is more") indicates a principle. The principle is simple: Schools cannot do everything; they must make choices. They need to decide what is most important and concentrate on that. When political leaders insist that all schools offer all sorts of courses and provide for all sorts of needs (needs that are often framed at the state and even national levels), then it follows that schools will have to be large.

But in the view of many people, the prevailing idea that schools must do everything is a mistake. It means that schools begin to look like franchise restaurants. They serve the same food everywhere, and this standardization serves local communities badly. Standardized educational products cannot respond well to local circumstances; standardized schools present generalized ideas that may not apply very well locally; and, often, such a school will provide less important (and perhaps more costly) services at the expense of more important services.

Staying small can mean that a school will be able to use resources to respond better to local circumstances. In fact, a great deal of recent research (see chapter 2) suggests that, although large schools try to do a multitude of things well, they often fail to deliver. The studies suggest that sheer size is probably a large contributing factor in this failure to deliver.

## Reestablishing Habits of Involvement

Long ago, rural schools were very small, localized, and directly controlled by citizens. The passing years have moved control of schools into the hands of professionals. While we are not suggesting a return to the old pattern, we do suggest that the trend has gone too far in isolating schools from the communities they serve.

**Problems of isolation.** Many problems spring from this isolation. Some parents may feel alienated and unwelcome at the school, especially if they are uncomfortable around college-educated teachers. This causes problems for the students, who must cross between the values and expectations of the home and those of the school. It can cause problems for teachers, who may feel that the parents don't care about and don't support their children's education. It causes problems for parents who feel that the school shuts them out, perhaps looks down on them, and is taking their children away from them.

However, schools and families share a common task. They have different information and different skills to bring to the task. The problem of isolation blocks accomplishment of their shared task, frustrating all those involved. How ironic that they should so often view one another as part of the problem rather than as partners.

The isolation of the school leads to other problems as well. It separates "school learning" from "life learning," and creates a false hierarchy of learning. One or both forms of learning may be slandered in the process. There are smart and successful people who scoff at "book learning," just as there are teachers and administrators who believe that the local culture presents barriers to school success.

In addition, the isolation of schools can create barriers to a community's full use of its investment in education. For example, consider the number of hours that many school buildings stand empty because school is viewed as fundamentally separate from other community functions. This description can apply even in a rural community that considers its school to be the center of its social life—especially when the social events that have created this impression are exclusively school-sponsored. In general, school buildings throughout America are not used to the extent that they could be used. And what applies to buildings applies also to human resources and activities.

Isolation of the school can also close the school off from community resources that might expand its curriculum and facilities. Does a small town need both a town park and a school playground, for example, or can the two units combine their funds to create one excellent facility? Does the 4-H program have a fine public speaking unit that could be offered to all students under the auspices of the school, stretching the capability of its language arts program? Imagine a rural community that combines all of its transportation needs into one bus system, funded by several sources, enabling elders to get to town and giving students and families more varied schedule options—including better access to after-school activities.

**Parents: There are no substitutes.** Parents and families are not only a child's first teacher, they are also a child's most *enduring* teacher. This is a significant and often overlooked fact.

Only at its worst does a child's home life encompass anything like the fragmentation of the school experience. Consider that experience: First, moving from adult to adult, year by year, each adult assuming a vast but temporary importance, and then—at the secondary level—moving through changing groups of adults and peers hour by hour throughout the day, and maybe even changing school buildings in the process. Who in this great rotation is watching out for the consistency and wholeness of the child's growth if not the family?

So the involvement of parents is inherent throughout the whole course of schooling—even if the parents never set foot in school. Obviously, though, increased contacts and cooperation between schools and parents could multiply the benefits of the continuity that parents and families provide in the upbringing and education of their children. More than a decade of research (see chapter 6) confirms this logic: Parent involvement increases student performance. It helps parents understand the expectations of teachers and the problems teachers face. It signals to the students that the school is not a separate world about which their parents know nothing. Equally important, however, parent involvement is a chance for teachers to learn more about the expectations, gifts, and problems of families—to learn more about their students and to express respect for children's lives outside of school.

**Bridging the gap.** Where small community schools differ from large ones is in their potential for bringing the community together around the school. Simply by virtue of size, small schools stand a better chance of creating consensus about their schools. They are prime candidates for involving parents and community members, because they know who those people are and where to find them. Small schools can readily find out what resources their community members hold—special knowledge, special experiences, talents, hobbies, and so forth.

In contrast to employers in urban areas, rural employers are likely to have employees whose children all attend one school, or at least schools in one system. Thus it behooves employers to pay attention to what happens in that school. It is also easier for the school and employer to identify ways to work together. A simple example might be letting parents out early on the day that the school is holding parent-teacher conferences.

Parent and community involvement in the schools can help create a shared vision toward which all can work. It can trim duplicated effort— much needed where resources are scarce. It can open up ideas for new ways that the school can meet community needs. Perhaps parents need parenting classes, or their own introduction to computers, or on-site child care in order to participate in activities with their older children. Parent involvement can open up ideas for new ways that the community can serve the purposes of the school—business apprenticeships, guest teachers, or financial assistance.

## Making Miracles

Under the U.S. system of government, the right and the responsibility to provide for schooling belong to the state. The state requires that children go to some acceptable form of school; parents cannot choose *not* to educate their children, though in many states they can choose home schooling. So, in the United States, citizens must conform to the state's insistence that children be schooled. But the fact that the state has the *responsibility* to provide for schooling also means that the state does not have the right to give up on certain portions of the population (for instance, the poor or the disabled) or to provide different levels and qualities of education to different groups on the basis of race, religion, or income. Citizens have the right to hold the state accountable for fulfilling this responsibility.

This is the context in which citizens can become advocates for education. Whether you are concerned with your own child's daily learning experiences, with the course offerings or teaching methods at your local school, or with the financial status or power politics of your school district, your participation is governed by the state's right and responsibility to educate children.

Nearly 200 years ago, a traveler from France, observing the youthful nation called the United States, remarked,

> These Americans are a peculiar people. If, in a local community, a citizen becomes aware of a human need that is not being met, he thereupon discusses the situation with his neighbors. Suddenly a committee comes into existence. The committee thereupon begins to operate on behalf of the need and a new community function is established. It is like watching a miracle, because these citizens perform this act without a single reference to any bureaucracy, or any official agency.
> —Alexis de Tocqueville

These miracles are still possible; they take place every day. Do not underestimate your contribution in this American context. You are already a citizen decision maker in your state's educational system. States differ from one another in their handling of major issues. They often make changes to their policies as a result of citizen opinion, and there is now a lot of ferment at the state level, ferment that is undoing much that has been taken for granted—for example, age-grading (e.g., grouping all 8-year-olds together in something called "the third grade"), norm-referenced testing (standardized achievement and IQ tests), and the assumption that bigger is always better.

CHAPTER 2

# Healthy Rural Schools, Good Rural Schools

What does good education look like? Opinions have varied greatly over the decades and centuries. One important fact to bear in mind, however, is that only since about 1850 has the expectation that everyone would go to some place called "school" been very widespread.

By 1900, however, almost all the white children in the United States were enrolled in elementary school. By 1965 almost all children in the nation were attending through high school. With more and more people going to places called "schools," we forget that even when there were very few schools, "education" still took place. Learning is something people just do—they learn to talk, they learn to do things, they learn to make things, and many have learned to read quite well—all without a formal system of schooling as we know it today.

Thus the question of what a good education looks like is not just a question of what you want to see happening in school. It's also a question about life—about what's important in this world and the commitments one makes (to family, to neighbors, to the land, to ideas, and so forth). There is no single right answer, then, to the question of what a good education looks like. Good education comes in many forms. It reflects differing assessments of what's important, different commitments, alternative ways to think about and encounter the world, and differing senses of personhood and community.

You can take on the mission of helping to decide what a good education is in your community and the best means of bringing that sort of education into your local school from the means at your disposal. This book aims to help you take account of many of the tools and ideas that really are at your disposal.

This chapter talks about knowledge of facts, development of skills, and understanding as important purposes of education. Basically, it argues (and you may not agree!) that *understanding* is the big picture into which facts and skills fit.

## The Balancing Act: What Does Education Accomplish?

Education is about the upbringing of children. Virtually all parents want to raise happy and capable children. We want our children to become responsible, skillful, competent, and caring adults. This is not an easy task. And the modern world makes it difficult in many ways. Most parents hold demanding jobs outside of the home, and people move around a lot so support networks are not what they used to be. People also play many roles during the course of a day: worker, parent, coach, cook, and counselor, to mention only a few. And the complexity of modern life increases as technology and commerce continue to shape and reshape how we work, with whom we work, and how wealth and income are created and distributed. New developments in the use of computers to communicate (telecommunications) are remaking the world, much as machines remade the world during the industrial revolution.

In this context, a good education is hard to find. It is even hard to define. Some observations are still possible, however. Education (whether good or ill) generally tries to help children

- acquire factual knowledge,
- develop skills, and
- understand the world.

Good education manages to do these three things well, but each educational domain—factual knowledge, skill, and understanding—represents difficult work for teachers and for students. One can argue, however, that *understanding the world* is the greatest challenge. Most schools concentrate on knowledge and skills, since it seems logical that *understanding the world* would depend on first acquiring knowledge and skills. Not so. Even small children possess an understanding of the world that develops naturally. If they did not, they could not learn to walk, climb steps, form meaningful sentences, or enjoy listening to books. In truth, understanding, skills, and knowledge depend on each other. We become more skillful as we understand better, and we understand better as we know more.

**Acquiring knowledge.** Traditionally, most people have believed that gaining factual knowledge is the most crucial and important part of schooling. For this reason, roughly 75 percent of classroom time continues to be devoted to imparting factual knowledge through lecturing, explaining, drilling, and testing. The person imparting knowledge, of course, is the teacher, and the familiar classroom arrangement is organized with the teacher as the center of attention. Thus the teacher's desk is traditionally positioned in the front of the classroom and rows of student desks are arranged facing the teacher.

There is no doubt that factual knowledge is important. But overemphasis on accumulating such knowledge can be a serious barrier to education! While facts and information are the easiest things to teach, they are also the easiest things to forget. If a student spends most of the day memorizing facts that are forgotten in a week or two (if not sooner), then precious time has been wasted. To be remembered, facts and information have to be attached (perhaps with the help of the teacher) to meaningful ideas. When facts and information are overemphasized, little time is left over for developing understanding or for using facts to do or make something. The sheer amount of information available in the contemporary world makes *overemphasizing* the acquisition of factual knowledge an obstacle to education.

Some may suggest that schools teach only the most important information. However, when any of us begins to choose which body of knowledge is most important, we bring into play ideas and commitments that help us make the choice. These are probably the same ideas and commitments we want our children to understand and adopt as they grow up. These ideas and commitments could be regarded as the core of a good education.

**Developing skills.** Skills are the routines and habits people develop in order to *do or make* something. Knowledge sits in the mind; skills bring knowledge out into the open where it can be seen. People develop skills by acquiring knowledge; and they develop knowledge by exercising their skills. And as people become more and more skillful, their understanding of the world changes in important ways. Someone who acquires information about cars and develops the skills to maintain and repair cars, for instance, is likely to understand the world as it relates to cars quite differently from someone who lacks such knowledge and skill.

Reading, writing, and mathematics are the basic academic skills that schools seek to develop. The only problem is that sometimes, perhaps too often, students get the idea that reading, writing, and math are deadly boring "subjects" and not essential tools for doing or making something. Part of the fault is that lessons often don't help students learn much about how these tools get used by real people. It's not that reading, writing, and mathematics are irrelevant to students' lives, but that many teachers are not themselves in a good position to reveal and emphasize that relevance to students, seldom having had firsthand experience in applying some of the skills they are expected to teach.

In addition to the basic skills, there are many other sorts of skills: athletic, social, mechanical, housekeeping, artistic, and even "thinking" skills. All of these sorts of skills can be learned in schools—if people think they are sufficiently important. Skills concern making and doing, rather than just knowing. Thinking skills, then, are directed at one sort of project or another—experiments, research reports, designs or plans, and analyses or summaries of ideas or events.

Skills are difficult to develop, and they are more difficult, therefore, to teach. It takes a lot of practice to get reasonably good at doing something. But perhaps this is the reason that skills usually last longer than any particular factual knowledge we acquire. Doing something or making something provides a framework that gives value to the related facts and information. Developing a skill, then, makes facts and information memorable.

Skills cannot be developed very well in a vacuum. Reading is not just an abstract operation—though it is often taught that way. The important thing about the skill of reading is its power to entertain, inform, or instruct us in our daily lives. Many people know how to read, but seldom read. That is why *reading aloud to young children* is so important: It shows them one of the purposes of reading—fun.

We have often made the mistake of trying to teach skills the way we have long taught knowledge—as if they were facts and information. We have fractured skills into small units, teaching the units in isolation and testing for mastery before moving on to the next small unit. This procedure actually drives knowledge and skill apart, rendering both meaningless. In some classrooms, this is what the overuse of worksheets can do.

**Understanding the world.** Even if schools routinely helped students put factual knowledge and skills together, it wouldn't be enough. Understanding the world is, by far, the most difficult thing to teach. Actually, understanding is not really directly *taught*. Instead, good teachers *elicit* understanding because students "come to an understanding" chiefly by putting things together for themselves. Good teachers help by nurturing, coaching, challenging, and sharing (their own understandings) with students.

In this sense, students "understand" when they grasp for themselves the meaning of their own lives in relationship to their families and communities, and when they have begun to grasp important ideas. This process of coming to understand begins at birth and goes on throughout life. Fulfilling

---

Box 2.1

Unlike verbal memories, something understood does not need to be exercised in order to be retained. This then, is the kind of learning that lasts for a lifetime and is of the greatest importance in the use of our minds and the conduct of our lives.

From: Adler, M. (1984). *The Paideia program: An educational syllabus*, p. 182. New York: Macmillan.

---

this part of the educational mission is not something that can be turned over entirely to the schools because it concerns commitments and judgments—meanings and values that extend far beyond the domain of the school.

Understanding is at least as useful as skills and knowledge. Think of understanding as a kind of navigational ability. Seeing the big picture—putting knowledge and skills together with commitments and ideas in a way that is meaningful—helps us move around successfully in the world. We know what's going on.

## Historical Shifts in Education Reform

For roughly 125 years, American public education has been moving away from small, citizen-controlled, rural schools toward large, professionally-controlled, urban schools. To be sure, this change represents a profound shift in Americans' understanding, not just of schooling, but of education itself. For better and for worse, today's complex system of schooling developed in response to specific historical forces. These forces included immigration, the rapid growth of cities, developments in science and technology and business, and Americans' appetite for more and more schooling. Just two generations ago, it was common for people not to finish the eighth grade. Today, it is uncommon for people not to finish high school. As a nation we are certainly more "schooled," and perhaps even better educated, than ever (see Box 2.2 for the comments of David Berliner, a thoughtful chronicler of teaching and learning in America).

It makes sense to stop and think about these changes—to consider whether what you have is really what you want. Does your school system serve the purposes of education as well as you want? In some communities, it does. But the arrival of the information age or postindustrial society has ushered in a period of intense scrutiny of our complex, large-scale system of schools. The number of reports that question the effectiveness of our schools—from various vantage points—would fill a library; and they have been accumulating for decades.

In fact, in the United States a system of schooling was designed to meet the requirements of the industrial age. As the industrial age draws to a

---

Box 2.2

**David Berliner on the Quality of American Education**

What may we reasonably conclude from these studies of standardized tests? First, there is no convincing evidence of a decline in standardized test performance. This is true of intelligence tests, the SAT, the NAEP (National Assessment of Educational Progress) tests, and the standardized achievement tests used by local school districts. If any case for change in these scores can be made, it is that the standardized aptitude and achievement test scores are going up, not down. Educators working under almost intolerable conditions in some settings have not as a group failed society. Rather, it appears that society has failed education. It is incredibly difficult to keep academic achievement constant or improve it with increasing numbers of poor children, unhealthy children, children from dysfunctional families, and children from dysfunctional neighborhoods. Yet the public school system of the United States has actually done remarkably well as it receives, instructs, and nurtures children who are poor, without health care, and from families and neighborhoods that barely function. Moreover,...they have done this with quite reasonable budgets too.

It is my belief that the American school system, as a whole, has been and continues to be a remarkable success. The campaign to discredit it and to blame it for the ills of our nation leads inevitably to making the wrong decisions about what to fix. Greater school improvement will come from providing poor people with jobs that pay enough to allow them to live with dignity, than from all the fooling around we can do with curriculum and instruction, or with standards and tests.... It is time for us to inform the politicians and business leaders of America that we cannot solve all the problems that they are creating. We will no longer take the blame for their actions. All of us in this nation must find ways to help each family live with dignity, so those families can give their children hope. Education is irrelevant to those without hope, and succeeds remarkably well for those who have it.

From: Berliner, D. (1993). Educational reform in an era of disinformation. *Education Policy Analysis Archives, 1*(2), 44-45.

---

close, the faults of this system have become more obvious to more people than ever before. But there have always been critics of the factory model of schooling, and for good reason.

The factory model was designed to sort students into *probable destinies*.

That is, the children of factory workers would get a form of schooling that would suit them to factory work, whereas the children of executives would get a form of schooling that would suit them to management roles. Almost all students were taught to be on time, to follow directions, and to tolerate boredom. The methods of managing schools were also imported directly from factories. People even began to talk about children as "the products" of the school. Most people now agree that following an industrial model has not promoted learning very well.

The point is *not* that we once had a good system of schooling, which has now grown out of date. On the contrary, one could argue that we made some dubious choices about education in the past; certainly, we need to rethink our choices now as people all over the world struggle to adjust to accelerated changes brought on by computers and other technology. Local rural communities can and should voice their concerns; greater variety in how schools are run and the commitments they reflect may well be part of a system that cultivates true education.

These days, one hears much talk about the need to design schools for the 21st century. Perhaps such talk means that instead of a factory model we need a computer model. In fact, the term being promoted these days for such schooling is the *virtual school* or even *hyperlearning*. The virtual school is a completely computerized school that may not even be housed in a school building but rather in people's homes, community centers, workplaces, and so forth. In the words of one commentator, virtual schooling will accomplish everything "faster, better, cheaper."[1]

It can sound exciting. But before making the switch to virtual schooling, we need to know more. The basic issue is not whether schooling uses all the latest inventions, but how well it cares for children and youth; how it ties knowledge, skills, and understanding together; and how it contributes to the quality of life in our families, communities, and the world at large. Some critics believe that schooling that merely follows the lead of technology—whether fashioned after factories or computers—is bound to end up as *mis*education.

Though the 21st century argument is too simple a view of schooling, many of the points raised in its defense have merit (see Box 2.3). Schools should make wise use of computer technology; it would be a good thing to nurture students' capacities to think; we do need instruction that integrates skills and knowledge; and our society would indeed be a better place if we nurtured thoughtfulness more widely.

---

[1] Perelman, L. (1992, December 10). *Hyperlearning: Clinton's greatest opportunity for change.* Discovery Institute Inquiry, pp. 1-12.

---

Box 2.3
**Schooling and the 21st Century (A View from 1986)**

Much of our system of elementary and secondary education evolved in the context of an economy based on mass production...

The skills needed now are not routine. Our economy will be increasingly dependent on people who...possess a feeling for mathematical concepts and the ways in which they can be applied to difficult problems, an ability to see patterns of meaning where others see only confusion; a cultivated creativity that leads them to new problems, new products, and new services...and...the ability to work with other people in complex organizational environments where work groups must decide for themselves how to get the job done.

Such people will...not come to the workplace knowing all they have to know, but knowing how to figure out what they need to know, where to get it, and how to make meaning out of it.

Success, then, depends on the whole society coming to place a much higher value not just on schooling but on learning. This demands a redefinition of the purposes of schooling, one that goes way beyond the inculcation of routine skills and the acquisition of a stock of facts. An economy based on people who think for a living requires schools dedicated to the creation of environments in which students become very adept at thinking for themselves, places where they master the art of learning and acquire a strong taste for it.

From: Carnegie Corporation of New York. (1986). *A nation prepared: Teachers for the 21st century* . The report of the Task Force on Teaching as a Profession. Hyattsville, MD: Carnegie Forum on Education and the Economy, pp. 15, 20-21.

---

What makes up a true education—good schooling as opposed to miseducation—consists of learning that, though of great value, was rationed out to only a small group in the past. In the late 19th and early 20th centuries, school leaders believed in a system of rationing, because it was thought that most people (including women and people of color) could never learn very much. Why waste resources on them? This view has moderated during the last half of the 20th century. The idea that all children are natural learners capable of a lot more than we can predict has taken hold in recent years.

Reading, writing, and mathematics have always been at the heart of a Western education, not as simple skills dissociated from the world, but as the means for gaining understanding and the background needed to negotiate the world. The most serious omission in the factory model was that it presented reading, writing, and mathematics as a set of fragmented skills taught in isolation from their use or enjoyment. In fact, the factory model demonstrated little respect for reading, writing, and mathematics. In essence, it ignored skill and understanding and concentrated on facts and information (knowledge). For too long, our instructional methods have emphasized "pouring in" knowledge. Our dominant method of teaching and of organizing schools and classrooms has emphasized passivity and content coverage (getting through the textbook) rather than the students' quest for understanding and meaning (see Box 2.4).

## Social and Political Forces Driving Consolidation

The modern approach to gaining "good education" has been played out most dramatically in rural America. Throughout the 20th century, American schools and school districts have been combined and recombined into ever larger units. This is a rural story because, until 1917, over 50 percent of Americans lived in rural areas: One-teacher and two-teacher schools (the 19th century model of schooling) went out of existence in droves.

The consolidation of rural schools, many scholars and citizens argue, contributes to the destruction of rural schools. Paul Theobald, a leading rural scholar, says flatly that America now has too few schools. Instead of consolidating and closing schools, he says, we should be building more schools and they should be small. Schools keep children in a community. And when they are small, and class sizes are smaller, more adults—adults who know, care about, and attend to them closely as *their community's children*—surround children, give them guidance, and are there to intervene when trouble comes.

The century-long school consolidation process corresponds closely to the industrial age and its characteristics: centralization, specialization, and standardization. In a sense, small *communities* during the 19th and 20th

---

Box 2.4
**New Literacies for Old**

The new literacy...goes beyond mere reading and writing ability...and beyond the current requirements for a high school diploma. It now includes capacities once demanded only of a privileged, college-bound elite: to think critically and creatively, solve problems, exercise judgment, and learn new skills and knowledge throughout a life time. What at the beginning of the twentieth century was a high standard for a few has apparently become, in the minds of a good many powerful people, a desideratum for all.

From: Brown, R. (1991). *Schools of thought: How the politics of literacy shape thinking in the classroom.* San Francisco: Jossey-Bass, pp. xii, xviii.

centuries were also consolidated into cities and suburbs. Urban creep remains a concern among rural places located near cities and suburban sprawl.

From the late 19th century onward, the password of schooling throughout America came to be *efficiency*. State laws and constitutions often contain language (adopted in the early 20th century) that calls for the government to maintain "thorough and efficient" systems of schooling. During virtually all of this time, schools in rural areas have been roundly criticized as inefficient, largely due to their small size. Time and again, it has been said that rural schools were too *small* to be efficient in purchasing equipment and supplies, providing scope for educational specialists, or offering a rich curriculum; too *isolated* to offer social stimulation or to attract and retain good teachers; and too *poor* to pay adequate salaries. The industrial-age solution? Make bigger rural schools.

And that is precisely what has happened, and continues to happen. In the 1949-1950 school year, 25.1 million children were enrolled in about 152,500 public schools. Forty years later, 40.5 million children were enrolled in about 84,600 public schools. That is, while the number of children in school *increased* by about 60 percent, the number of schools *decreased* by about 45 percent! During this time period, in fact, about 60,000 one-teacher schools (mostly in rural areas) were closed.[2]

In essence, rural schools have been made to get in line with the norm for urban and suburban areas. Yet, rural schools in most places are still much smaller than the schools in urban and suburban areas. On that basis, in fact, they are *still* too often judged to be deficient: The supposed negatives of rural schools seem to persist no matter what. The opinion often—though not by any means always—held by state officials is that a small rural school cannot offer a good education.

The story of private schooling should cause us to question this view. During the same years that small public schools in rural areas were being closed, small private schools were opening. Between 1949-1950 and 1989-1990, the number of private schools *doubled*. And their enrollments are much smaller than in public schools. In all locations, from urban to rural, private schools are much smaller than public schools containing the same grades.

The contrast between public and private school size is extreme at the high school level. Conventional thinking says high school enrollments need to be really large—at least 1,000 students in many accounts. How-

[2] Grymes, J. A., & Harwarth, I. B. (1992). *Historical trends: State education facts, 1969-1989.* Washington, DC: National Center for Education Statistics. (ERIC Document Reproduction Service No. ED 351 366)

ever, 47 percent of private schools containing a 12th grade enroll *fewer than 150 students*. The similar figure for public schools is 14 percent. Even in urban areas, 40 percent of private high schools enroll fewer than 150 students and only 12 percent enroll more than 750. But 66 percent of public high schools enroll more than 750 students in urban areas. Small size is considered a distinct advantage among educators and parents involved with private schools. There is little doubt that small private schools can offer a good education; likewise, small, rural *public* schools can offer a good education. What they can't do in a cost-efficient manner is look and act like smaller-scaled versions of comprehensive metropolitan middle and high schools.

Rural citizens usually understand consolidation, but it commonly creates crisis in rural areas. Frequently, the community regards its school possessively, believing the school belongs to the community. However, court cases and laws take a much different view. Again and again, state legislatures and courts—and even the U.S. Supreme Court[3]—have made it clear that legislatures and state departments of education have the right to create and disband school *districts* and that local school boards have a similar right to create and close *schools*. School districts and school attendance areas—unlike counties, townships, or towns—are not viewed as governmental regions in which citizens' rights are officially granted. A state may provide in law that decisions to close a school be put before the voters, but this provision is not commonplace.

Of course, attempts by the state or local school board to close schools are sometimes effectively countered by community members. In these cases, however, the community either convinces the involved decision makers that practical alternatives exist, or they bring sufficient power to bear that the plans are abandoned. Often, of course, both tactics come into play when consolidation moves are defeated.

The next part of this chapter gives you information about alternatives to consolidation, all based on solid studies of key issues related to school size. Chapter 5 considers the issue of power—that is, getting organized to make a forceful case. But before you consider any of these matters—before you choose sides—you first have to take hold of the issue and *understand* it. Sometimes consolidation makes sense for communities! It always makes some kind of sense to somebody; it is important to find out what sense it makes, and to whom. Taking hold of the consolidation issue means informing yourself about the relationship between school size and the quality of programs offered, about what factors influence student achievement (what they learn) and attainment (how far they advance through the

---

[3] Example: Gong Lum v. Rice, 48 S. Ct. 91 (1928).

school system), and about the financial circumstances affecting rural schools.

If you seriously wish to see the school(s) in your community offer children a good education, then you will want to consider the situation objectively. Acknowledge your school's weak spots, identify its strengths, seek options open-mindedly, and develop plans tailored to your community's unique blend of need, circumstance, and values.

Before proceeding further, we need to point out the connection between consolidation as a local issue and consolidation as a *state policy*. *Consolidation* commonly arises within a community because it has already been favored as a policy at the state level. But state departments do not necessarily spell out this policy directly. They may even deny that they have such a policy. But where there are financial incentives and special services offered to districts or schools that consolidate, where there is a funding formula that favors larger schools, where there are guidelines for "optimal school size," where there is undue attention paid to certain large schools as "models" for the state, there may well be a consolidation agenda at the state level—a policy climate that favors the creation and maintenance of large schools.

In order to appreciate the scope of a state's responsibility, you should know that the federal constitution says *nothing* about education. Schooling in the United States is what is known as a "reserved right." Because the U.S. constitution is silent about education, the right and responsibility for schooling is a matter for each state. This is not the case in many nations, and, in the United States, this situation has created a system that is very different from, say, the French or Japanese or German systems.

The individual state in the United States is responsible for conducting schooling as fairly as possible and for ensuring the quality of education. Furthermore, in many states (particularly in the South) it bears most of the responsibility for actually funding the school system. The state's right to create policies toward these ends cannot be challenged (see Box 2.5).

States consolidate schools and districts, in large part, because policy makers firmly believe that *economies of scale* save money and improve schools. *Economies of scale* is a business concept. The idea is that larger units result in greater purchasing power and increased opportunities to streamline production (for example, through specialization). This sort of thinking leads to schools that resemble one another in many ways, wherever you go. Differences persist, of course, but when all schools are held to very similar standards, the extent of those differences (both good and bad) are held in check. Large scale, for some people, is a tool for reducing variability. That's part of what *standardization* means.

Small rural schools, however, especially need the latitude to develop ways to work with their communities to offer the kind of schooling that

---

Box 2.5
**The Expanding Role of State Government**

In recent years, under the leadership of the nation's governors, state influence has increased. Recent initiatives at the national level (for example, development of the National Education Goals, the provisions of the Goals 2000 legislation, the movement toward national standards for various school subjects, and new efforts in assessment and data-gathering) are likely to increase this influence. In this context, it is more important than ever before that the voice of community members and local educators be heard. Most officials recognize this fact, but providing for that voice to be heard is also a community's responsibility to itself.

---

nurtures a good education. They can do this on their own terms in ways that minimize their weaknesses and maximize their strengths—if communities and educators make plans together and work productively with the state agencies that set many of the rules that schools in a given state are supposed to follow.

Momentous social and economic changes accompany the end of the industrial age. A lot of work and thought is going into defining what good education looks like. These trends, we believe and hope, combine to create a context in which small rural schools can make a much greater impact on their students and their communities than at any time in the past 30 years. But first of all, schools must know what community they are serving and by what criteria they will be judged—both by that community and by the state.

States are not generally disposed to see things from the perspective of a local community; indeed, local communities are often portrayed as "enemies of progress" when they oppose consolidation. But you and your neighbors, working together, can help clarify the real effects of policies and suggest alternatives to policy makers. Officials *can* be educated, and they are usually susceptible to effectively organized public opinion.

It is true that most of the *official* rights lie with state departments of education and local school boards. Concerted public opinion and action works *unofficially*, which actually means you have a wider array of purposes, strategies, and tactics at your disposal. It may also mean that you can respond more quickly and more vigorously than can most state agencies.

**Consolidation on the local level.** What does consolidation on the state agenda mean for you on the local level? Depending on the degree of pressure from the state, it is likely to mean one or more of the following things:

- Your local board may be under extreme pressure to follow the state's agenda, regardless of local opinion or the specifics of the local situation.

- Since the consolidation issue often evokes a strong emotional response, your community will be inclined to polarize over this issue rather than to take the time and effort to study what is best, given the facts.

- Through creating the agenda, those who favor consolidation will have a powerful advantage over those who wish to study the situation and those who oppose consolidation.

- It may be necessary to challenge state-level assumptions in order to create a climate in which local deliberations can proceed openly and creatively.

- It is up to your community to do your local homework, relating your particular situation to the policy. By their very nature, statewide policies have difficulty accounting for local circumstances, which can vary tremendously within a single state.

A state policy that promotes consolidation will likely mask the difference between issues directly related to school size and issues related to *ruralness*. A study of small schools in New York State, for instance, concluded that "none of the organizational alternatives we studied can eliminate the extra cost of providing education in rural settings."[4] Population sparsity (ruralness) is what necessitates small schools in rural areas; making bigger schools involves added transportation costs, for instance, and students can be transported only so far. In other words, providing the same services in rural areas as those provided elsewhere almost always costs more money. Consolidation is not necessarily a cost-saving measure.

Consolidation on the local level involves a lot of issues: the role of the school as a social center; the effects on the jobs of community members (bus drivers, teachers, administrators, custodians); parents' concern for the well-being of their children; power struggles among interest groups; and differing views of what a good education might be.

When consolidation crops up as a proposal, it usually divides communities. Often communities polarize into the pros and the cons, with professional educators and some community members generally favoring the plan, and other community members and some professional educators opposing it. In general, consolidation efforts have been undertaken with guidance from the education profession. This doesn't mean that all local

---

[4]Monk, D. H., & Haller, E. J. (1986). *Organizational alternatives for small rural schools. Final report to the legislature of the state of New York.* Ithaca, NY: Cornell University. (ERIC Document Reproduction Service No. ED 281 694)

teachers and administrators fall in line with professional consensus. In fact, the consensus is changing, and many leading educators have become firm supporters of the need to create and maintain small schools (see Box 2.6).

Obviously, this handbook is not intended as a tool for people who want to make schools larger! Neither is it intended as a tool for people who want to ignore the important facts and ideas concerning consolidation and school size generally. Consolidation and school closings are usually painful for many people. But sometimes it will make sense to close a school.

The point is that closures should take place for good reasons, and in giving the reasons and developing plans (including alternatives to closure), community members should be active and knowledgeable partners. The last section of this chapter is intended to help educators and community members access the knowledge they need about consolidation and school size. This knowledge is part of what you need to know in order to assess your local situation. It is not about how to organize for action (see chapter 5 for a discussion of getting organized).

## Bigger May Not be Better: Addressing the "Hard" Issues

Whether consolidation involves a rural school or a school district, the issues on which people build their arguments are quite similar. Those who favor consolidation stress financial efficiency, improvement of facilities, and increased breadth of course offerings. Those who oppose consolidation stress small class size, school climate, and student and family participation.

School consolidation is usually promoted as school reform, and the underlying presumption (until recently) has been that "bigger is better." According to researchers David Monk and Emil Haller, school reform concerns can be roughly divided into "hard" and "soft" issues.[5] Hard issues include student achievement (for instance, standardized test scores); breadth and depth of course offerings; increased accountability for professional staff; and higher salaries for teachers. Soft issues focus more on the social aspects of schools: school climate, extracurricular participation, parent involvement, and decentralized decision making.

One reason that those who oppose consolidation often lose the political fight may be that they do not adequately address the "hard" issues emphasized by the other side—course offerings, costs, and achievement. Instead,

---

[5] Haller, E. J., & Monk, D. H. (1988, Nov). New reforms, old reforms, and the consolidation of small rural schools. *Educational Administration Quarterly, 24*(4), 470-483.

Box 2.6
SERGIOVANNI, GOODLAD, BOYER, AND HUSÉN
On Small Schools

Each of these excerpts was written by a renowned national school reformer (that is, not by someone particularly dedicated to rural schools or to preserving small schools). Ernest Boyer and John Goodlad are both widely known and respected for many studies about what schools are like and how to improve them; Torsten Husén is an internationally known scholar whose specialty is student achievement research; and Thomas Sergiovanni's specialty is school leadership and supervision.

**Boyer, E. (1983). *High school: A report on secondary education in America*. Philadelphia: Harper & Row.**

Large schools include a substantial group of "outsiders," students with poor academic records and no extracurricular involvement, a group almost unknown in small schools. (p. 234)

It is difficult to say when a school is too big, the point where schools-within-a-school should be introduced. We do suggest, however, that schools enrolling 1,500 to 2,000 students are good candidates for reorganization into smaller units of several hundred each. (p. 235)

Large high schools...should reorganize themselves into smaller units...to establish a more cohesive, more supportive social setting for all students. (pp. 314-315)

**Goodlad, J. (1984). *A place called school: Prospects for the future*. New York: McGraw-Hill.**

It is not impossible to have a good large school; it is simply more difficult. What are the defensible reasons for operating an elementary school of more than a dozen teachers and 300 boys and girls? I can think of none. (p. 309)

Indeed, I would not want to face the challenge of justifying a senior, let alone junior, high of more than 500 to 600 students. (p. 310)

Recent research summaries raise fundamental questions about the assumed cost and programmatic advantages of increased school size, especially when weighed against disadvantages such as increased anonymity of students and greater impersonality in the student-teacher relationship. (p. 338)

**Husén, T. (1985). The school in the achievement-oriented society: Crisis and reform. *Phi Delta Kappan, 66*(6), 398-402.**

In a system in which individuals are familiar with one another, social relations can remain informal; those who break the rules are easily identified and subjected to social sanctions. But in a large organization—one in which individuals do not know everyone else— an elaborate system of rules and formal proceedings replaces the informal, social means of control. At the same time, the size and complexity of the organization force it to become hierarchical. (p. 400)

Large schools with formally structured social contacts tend to fragment students' contact with adults in the schools.... Instruction becomes increasingly divided among teachers with specialized competencies.... Different aspects of individual children are parceled out among the specialists. (p. 400)

One of the consequences of fragmented caretaking with compartmentalized services is that children become reluctant to "invest" in a particular adult. When this happens, discipline problems ensue. (p. 400)

We must take steps to make schools smaller. (p. 401)

Most [real] education occurs in small, close communities.... In urban, bureaucratized society, more attention is paid to the superficial qualities of individuals than to deeper character traits, which can be discovered only through close and prolonged contact. This is also true of schooling, and any attempt to come to grips with today's troubled schools must consider how to establish more self-directed schools with closer ties to parents and to the surrounding community. (p. 402)

**Sergiovanni, T. (1993, April). *Organizations or communities? Changing the metaphor changes the theory.* Paper presented at the annual meeting of the American Educational Research Association, Atlanta, GA. (ERIC Document Reproduction Service No. ED 376 008)**

Community...will mean the dissolution of the high school as we now know it into several small schools rarely exceeding 300 or so students.... Elementary schools would have to give serious consideration to organizing themselves into smaller and probably multiaged families. (pp. 17-18) they stick to the "soft" issues. As a result, their arguments do not hit the opposition convincingly; and, remember, the ones who are behind most calls for consolidation are people in state agencies, people with the *right* to decide if a school should be closed or if districts should be combined. Arguments put to state and local education agencies and to school boards and officials *need to be convincing.* A politically strong case for retaining schools in small rural communities, therefore, needs to handle the "hard" issues directly and creatively.

This section of the chapter challenges some of the assumptions of the bigger-is-better mentality with the results of research studies. We have tried to make this a straightforward discussion that anybody can understand. One thing may not be obvious, though: The hard issues of school finance cannot be separated from the finances of families or from local economic conditions. We suggest, therefore, that some of the "hard" issues are not being considered in their proper context. For example, removing schools from local communities may, on one hand, result in some short-term savings, but the closing may also weaken the potential for community improvement or even survival. On the other hand, getting the community involved to make the school a better place would be a worthy investment—for the community and its children. There is a similar connection between most of the "soft" issues and one or more of the "hard" issues.

One final warning. Most communities are not going to make their decision solely on the basis of research findings, nor should you. You must also consider the goals and values of your community, and how the research relates to your particular situation. But research can help you get beyond the unexamined arguments with which consolidation schemes are sometimes defended. More important, in the long run, it can help you explore what will really best serve your children and your community.

**Course offerings.** One common justification for consolidating schools is the assumed need to expand high school course offerings. The charge is made that small high schools cannot provide a curriculum with adequate breadth and depth to meet students' diverse needs.

David Monk and colleagues at Cornell University are perhaps the experts on this topic.[6] They suggest that the curriculum argument for consolidation has been significantly overstated. In general, a total high school enrollment of 400 students is enough to allow a high school to provide an adequately broad and deep curriculum. Increases in the size of

---

[6] Monk, D. H., & Haller, E. J. (1993, Spring). Predictors of high school academic course offerings: The role of school size. *American Educational Research Journal, 30*(1), 3-21.

very small schools produce greater gains than increases in the size of larger schools. Thus, increasing enrollment from 100 to 200 may make a big difference; increasing from 200 to 400 will probably make less of a difference; and increases above 400 are uneven in the schools studied.

Monk and colleagues also note that a school enrollment above 400 merely presents the *opportunity* to provide a rich curriculum. It does not ensure actual provision. In other words, whether or not a high school provides an adequately broad and deep curriculum depends on leadership.

Whatever the size of the school, schools can offer appropriate courses that meet evident needs (depending on the characteristics of communities and students) or, as is not uncommon in this research, they can fail to do so. The 400-student threshold merely makes it easier for good leadership to fulfill its responsibilities with respect to depth and breadth of course offerings.

But the nature of an "adequate" curriculum is also at issue. The national studies suggest one standard: The presence of a range of specialized academic and vocational courses from remedial to advanced levels. For communities operating very small high schools (particularly those with fewer than 400 students), the suburban sort of high school may not respond to local circumstances. For instance, a much more narrowly focused academic curriculum can produce high levels of achievement even when enrollments are quite small. This model may account for the success of Catholic high schools, which, even in urban areas, are much smaller than their public counterparts.

Thus, while variety of course offerings is a serious issue, you need to be aware that offering a larger number of courses is only marginally related to offering a good education. Why? There is little relationship between the number of courses a school offers and overall student achievement. There are several reasons for this. First, in many cases, additional course offerings are not advanced courses in core academic subjects. Instead, they may be remedial or enrichment courses. Second, relatively few students take advantage of the additional courses, whether advanced, remedial, or enrichment. Third, nothing guarantees that more course offerings lead to a well-coordinated and well-conceived curriculum, where one course leads directly to another, and where the overall program fits together in ways that make sense. There is a difference between offering a smorgasbord and ensuring that people eat a well-balanced meal. Finally, the number of courses offered has no relationship to the quality of instruction. Challenging students widely and deeply with fewer well-taught courses, which together form a coherent whole, will advance their learning a good deal more than an unrelated assortment.

All of this suggests that the number of course offerings is much too vague a yardstick for assessing the worth of a curriculum. Instead, you need to assess your actual offerings against state requirements, against core programs in other schools, and against the expectations of the community, including the community's expectations for postsecondary education. Does your school, indeed, lack some important courses (like foreign languages and advanced courses in math and science)? You need to see if everything fits together in a way that makes sense ("curriculum coordination"), particularly in a way that makes sense in light of local circumstances.

There are a lot of questions to consider when the issue is curriculum, and the easy notion that just offering more courses is the best course of action is a hazardous simplification (see Box 2.7 for some questions to ask).

**Student achievement.** The positive effects of small school size on students' attitudes and satisfaction, extracurricular participation, attachment to school, and attendance have been confirmed by decades of research findings, according to William Fowler, a researcher with the National Center for Education Statistics. That is, the "soft" issues of school reform as it relates to small size are definitely confirmed by research.

But studies continue to examine the unique influence of school and district size on student achievement. Early studies (from 1924 to 1974) that examined school size tried to answer the question, "What is the best size for elementary schools and high schools?" The answer depended, however, on what was used to judge "the best." Some studies looked at "input" (for example, costs and teachers' credentials), whereas others looked at "output" (for example, achievement). Input studies determined that schools needed to be about twice the size determined by output studies. But, even the early studies did not recommend dramatic increases in school size as a means of improving student achievement.

During the past decade, researchers have continued to study achievement as it relates to school size. When all else is held equal, comparisons of schools and districts based on differences in enrollment generally favor smaller units. The key phrase here is "when all else is held equal." Thanks to new technologies and improved data collections, researchers can now sort out the influence of school size from other powerful influences, such as family resources and previous levels of student achievement. Such research techniques were not available to previous generations of observers. The earlier studies tended not to find much difference at all in the achievement of students in small and large schools.

The newer studies, employing better methods, however, uncover a negative relationship between school (or district) size and student achievement. That is, the lower the enrollment, the higher the achievement. The advantage to small schools might come from the effect of small size on the

---

Box 2.7
## Questions for Curriculum Development

• How do people want to challenge students to grow and learn?

• What are the goals for students?

• What commitments will the community make?

• Does the community want to send more children to college?

• Does the community want to see fewer children in remedial courses?

• Can some courses be done away with?

• Can scheduling patterns change for the better?

• Can counseling be changed to help students take more challenging courses?

---

achievement of disadvantaged students. One 1993 study of students in Alaska found that small elementary schools benefitted disadvantaged students most by making poverty and other challenges less of a factor in school achievement.[7] A 1988 study of achievement in California schools and districts found that students in low-income communities performed *much better* in small schools, whereas students in high-income communities performed *somewhat better* in large schools.[8] Logic suggests that if there are more low-income communities in a state than high-income communities, overall achievement will be better if schools are smaller.

Most studies have relied on standardized achievement tests, which attempt to measure students' basic skills. But maybe these tests are overlooking other important learning. One 1993 study investigated whether or not large schools do a better job teaching higher-order thinking skills than do small schools.[9] With higher-order thinking items as the measure of achievement, the researchers found no significant difference in the performance of students in small rural high schools and larger high schools in more urbanized areas. (See chapter 6 for further descriptions of the studies described here.)

---

[7] Huang, G., & Howley, C. B. (1993). Mitigating disadvantage: Effects of small-scale schooling on students' achievement in Alaska. *Journal of Research in Rural Education, 9*(3), 137-149.

[8] Friedkin, N., & Necochea, J. (1988). School system size and performance: A contingency perspective. *Educational Evaluation and Policy Analysis, 10*(3), 237-249.

[9] Haller, E., Monk, D., & Tien, L. (1993). Small schools and higher-order thinking skills. *Journal of Research in Rural Education, 9*(2), 66-73.

---

Box 2.8
Doing a Few Things Well

The search for a reasonable set of core courses is one of the hallmarks of the current education reform movement nationwide. It is fascinating to see both conservative documents...and liberal reports...all united by their call for a narrower, more unified and focused curriculum.... Although they...differ considerably on the specific content, no one is advocating the idea that more courses, more options, more tracks, and more of a "cafeteria" approach to curriculum will enhance educational quality. This emerging national consensus on the need for a leaner, stronger curriculum...means that small rural high schools, in particular, can no longer be complacent about the "gaps" in their ability to provide students with first-rate instruction in all essential areas.... Most important, however, this trend in educational reform should give small rural schools a new lease on life and a renewed sense of their own capacity for educational excellence.... Small, rural schools should thrive in an era that honors a limited, focused, well-rounded curriculum.... When a premium is placed on doing a few things well, rather than trying to be all things to all people, small rural schools are in a position to compete successfully with larger systems—and to excel.

From: Sher, J. P. (1988). *Class dismissed: Examining Nebraska's rural education debate,* p. 15. Chapel Hill, NC: Rural Education and Development. (ERIC Document Reproduction Service No. ED 305 194)

---

Apparently, then, it *is* true that some of the things private schools claim to do well, small public schools (probably with a more financially challenged group of students) are also doing well. This news, however, is hardly ever celebrated. That doesn't make the contributions of small rural schools less real (see Box 2.8).

**Economies of scale (financial efficiency).** Our society is based on a successful commitment to free trade and enterprise. According to Jane Jacobs, who studies the economies of urban and rural areas, the fundamental values that energize this commitment include ease, convenience, and low cost. Efficiency in production and marketing translates these values into reality.

All sorts of economies are realized by conducting business on a sufficiently large scale: economies in purchasing, administration, assembly, shipping, marketing—the list goes on and on. The location of a business plays a part, as well. When business people consider their options, they actively scout sites for their operations. And rural areas often find themselves in competition with one another for firms seeking favorable offers. In the end, businesses locate their operations in the places that offer the most advantages.

When schooling is viewed as a production process in the context of the normal operation of the free-enterprise system, it is natural enough to point to the importance of "economies of scale." Production facilities in any line of business need to be a certain size (generally, not too large and not too small) to manufacture things efficiently. From this point of view, why should it be any different with schooling?

In fact, if schooling is like production, then (up to some upper limit), the larger the school, the lower the cost per student. Many studies of schooling have compared expenditures per student among schools of different size. The studies invariably find that more must be spent per student in small schools, especially the very smallest. Of course, few such studies were done in the 19th century. Most school funding at that time was entirely local; there was no way to gather the data; and the tools of statistical analysis were not really invented until early in the 20th century. All we can know is that, today, the smaller schools that remain in operation seem to cost more per pupil in comparison to larger schools. But we also know that per-student costs begin to increase after a certain size is reached. The largest schools (principally in the largest cities) prove to be very expensive to operate per student.

Something funny is going on in such studies. Part of that "something" is the idea that schooling is like the business of manufacturing. Schools, in fact, offer no literal product; they don't literally distribute graduates to eager buyers; and they certainly do not have the option of developing their operations in the most favorable location. The state says that children *must* go to school, no matter where they live, and no matter how unfavorable their living conditions may be for learning. They have to go, and the state must provide schools.

When studies find that very small schools and very large schools are inefficient in terms of per-student expenditures, they are not just looking at an effect of size—though that is how the findings are usually understood. They are also looking at a number of effects of poverty.

Inner cities and rural areas have poverty rates that are about equal. In the cities, the standard bigger-is-better view created immense schools—many thousands of children and young people in a single facility. The sheer size of these inner-city schools seems to make it a lot more difficult for teachers to claim the attention and nurture the learning of those who attend. These difficulties are compounded by inner-city poverty.

In rural areas, the bigger-is-better view has also reshaped education as one-teacher schools—which kept schools close to homes—have all but vanished. Transportation is a major issue in most rural school districts; buses and drivers are expensive. Sparsity of population is a challenge unique to rural areas. So, many rural schools are still quite small by urban and suburban standards. Efficiently operating the array of programs mandated by the state and federal governments is difficult. And, again, these difficulties are compounded by poverty, particularly in terms of the tax base, which generally falls well short of the suburban and urban norm. One advantage, however, is that the smaller size of rural schools often seems to blunt the *personal* effects of poverty (as achievement studies suggest). The fact is, rural schools face extra costs for serving a sparse population, no matter how they organize their schools. If schooling were a business dependent on volume of sales to a local population, it might not choose to locate in a rural area.

The difficulty with the metaphor of "economies of scale"—the comparison it makes between business (particularly manufacturing) operations and schooling—is that it breaks down beyond a superficial level. Children are not assembled from raw materials; they are not designed and redesigned for the convenience of consumers; they are not shipped, marketed, and closed out when outmoded. Taking this business comparison too seriously does damage to children and to the very idea of a good education.

The claim has been made for nearly 100 years that creating bigger schools saves taxpayer money, principally through the "economies of scale" achieved in consolidated units. The evidence offered, however, has always been the results of studies comparing *existing* schools of different size. The claim is made, "Look how expensive these small schools and districts are! And look how much less expensive (per student) these large schools and districts are! If we want to save money, we need to make our schools and districts larger." The argument is that simple, and, as we have seen, it usually prevails. But there is a big problem with this thinking. What if something in the environment (say, population sparsity, increased transportation costs, or poverty) keeps the larger schools and districts created from the smaller schools and districts from actually realizing the projected savings? This possibility is not usually considered.

In fact, few studies have actually compared the cost of running a consolidated school to the costs of running the smaller schools from which it was made. This is probably not just an oversight. First, the usual argument is so often used that no one—especially those directly responsible for closing any particular school—wants to confront the possibility of error. In the midst of controversy, no one wants "independent observers" mucking about in potentially embarrassing information. Second, the issue of consolidation also has to do with control—many small schools are a lot more difficult to control administratively than a few large ones. In all the history of consolidation, a hidden agenda may actually have been set by the growing number of school administrators who led the fight for larger schools, and whose careers and destiny as a group benefitted. And third, it is difficult to do such before-and-after studies, which require detailed school-level finance information. That information is not often compiled in routine and reliable ways at the school level.

What about an optimal size for schools, though? If it seems that, in ideal circumstances, schools can be too small, and that—again, in ideal circumstances—schools can be too large, isn't there some size (in ideal circumstances) that would be just right? If America were an evenly populated country, if it were not the most culturally diverse nation in the world, if there were not great extremes of wealth and poverty, if the circumstances of knowledge and meaning were not so changeable, and maybe if America were a smaller nation with schooling organized at the national level—then maybe there would be an optimal size.

We have many different types of schools; all the possible combinations of grades are actually grouped together and called schools; all races and ethnic groups attend those schools; we have 50 different state systems of education (plus territorial authorities); we have extremely affluent and extremely impoverished communities; and we live in a society in the midst of an information and knowledge explosion. In all this creative confusion, there is definitely *no optimal size*. If there were an optimal size today, it would be created by figuring an average of very, very different circumstances; and it would be out of date tomorrow (see Box 2.9).

While research shows that school smallness does not automatically

---

Box 2.9
**Optimal Size:  Fantasizing a Moving Target**

In the case of efficiency, we looked at the extensive literature on economies of scale. We concluded that although large schools may offer such economies, they also face diseconomies of scale, and that the point of balance between these two is entirely unclear and idiosyncratic. Perhaps one of the most enduring bits of wishful thinking in the reorganization folklore concerns the notion of an optimal size for school districts. That notion is pure fantasy.

Monk, D. H., & Haller, E. J. (1986). *Organizational alternatives for small rural schools. Final report to the legislature of the state of New York*, p. 78. Ithaca, NY: State University of New York. (ERIC Document Reproduction Service No. ED 281 694)

result in inefficiency or failure to offer a good education, it also does not automatically mean that small schools are good. Small schools do seem to have certain advantages, but there is no guarantee that any particular small school is actually *realizing* these advantages. As we hope this section of the chapter suggests, making a school better is more a question of minimizing disadvantages and maximizing advantages than just hoping that the usual odds apply (see Box 2.10).

In some small schools, the curriculum may well be impoverished and inadequate, student achievement poor, and operations financially inefficient. But these qualities certainly do not apply to most small schools. On the contrary, the odds suggest that nothing inherent in small size—even for high schools with enrollments less than 150 students—makes a good education unlikely. The research also suggests that the benefits generally claimed for consolidation and school closure have been consistently exaggerated.

## Deciding About Consolidation

Very few rural communities are self-sufficient in the way that they might once have been. They are certainly less isolated and more dependent on commerce and communications with other places than they were in the 19th century. Political disputes on the other side of the globe can affect local communities in the United States rather quickly. Virtually every local community has a higher degree of involvement with a larger, less predictable sphere than was the case 100 or even 30 years ago. Control— local or otherwise—has become a complex issue. So what?

---

Box 2.10
**Maximizing the Odds**

Smallness, to be effective, must be accompanied by at least one other element:...sufficient autonomy to use one's smallness to advantage. It doesn't do us much good to know each other well if we can't use that knowledge. Nor do adults modeling good discourse serve much point if the discourse is only about the details, not ever about the big picture. Loyalties aren't engendered in schools that can't protect their own, that are controlled by rules that view adults and children as so many interchangeable parts.

From: Meier, D. (1995). *The power of their ideas: Lessons for America from a small school in Harlem*, p. 115. Boston: Beacon Press.

So, your community and others probably have an identity crisis to resolve. This is part and parcel of making decisions about the community school. For example, are you maintaining a community that exists only as a school community—one that doesn't exist much beyond that bond? If so, do you still wish to maintain it? Can the school become the centerpiece of efforts to create more of a community than exists at present? Or does your real, active community follow different lines than those that surround the school? Would you be better off to realign your school with the boundaries of that community so that it truly becomes a community school? Might this, in your case, involve consolidating in some way with another school in the area?

Small *is* different. As you tackle a decision about consolidation, be clear about this fact. You can't have it both ways. If you want to do things the way large urban and suburban schools do, consolidation may well be a good choice. But that choice is not the only option. Small schools can use the strengths of smallness to provide excellent education. In fact, small schools offer the very advantages that large schools now seek to create through such options as a school-within-a-school and multi-age student groups. Small schools in a community setting offer the further advantage of being better able to fully use their community and locale as a teaching environment. They have a richer classroom just outside their doors than any indoor classroom anywhere.

Getting there from here requires you to claim your difference from the urban norm and to train yourselves as teachers, community members, administrators, and students to do things differently. Growing social interest in more personal, human-scaled institutions, as well as national trends toward local (or site-based) decision making, suggest that small, rural schools can enter a new era of promise—promise that can only be fulfilled school by school, community by community.

## Beyond Your Community: State Policy and You

State policy affects local options dramatically, so any serious look at consolidation will almost always lead back to a state's education policies. States turn to consolidation to solve problems, though many people feel that consolidation creates as many problems as it solves. Nonetheless, if you wish to affect state policy, you will need to have something positive to offer in place of school consolidation, or you will simply be viewed as someone blocking progress.

While it is beyond the scope of this book to suggest statewide policies, some characteristics of alternative policies are clearly evident in the book's underlying ideas. Moreover, such suggestions are provided in

Monk and Haller's research report to the New York State Legislature[10] and the alternatives to consolidation are considered at greater length in a report by E. Robert Stephens.[11]

You need to be aware that in many states, consolidation is a *de facto* rural education policy; for the most part, states do not have special policies for rural schools and districts. Such a policy might avoid the use of consolidation as a general policy instrument for improving small rural schools. We want to point out three features of a more suitable rural education policy.

**Integrated services.** This idea refers to providing a variety of social services—such as health, education, and job-training—under one umbrella. Many schools already offer a variety of social services: free and reduced-price meals, hearing and vision tests, health screening, and fluoride treatments are common examples. School-based clinics that would offer a full range of health care to students would go a step further.

State policy could support a community's efforts to find ways of combining such services. Taking this approach does not mean that schools would take on more and more tasks and responsibilities! The idea is that schools and other services work together much more closely to serve the community. Local boards that oversee these services, such as the board of education, might jointly hire an administrative team to see to the daily provision of the services. This approach would emphasize the integrity of the community over the separateness of services (for example, education and health services). The more common approach, we note, is to share administration across geographical lines rather than across service lines, as when two communities share one school superintendent.

**Improved course offerings.** If the state wants to see increased course offerings in rural schools, its policies can recognize and nurture a number of options, such as providing access to satellite learning services, fostering within- or between-district distance-learning ventures, and operating advanced-studies centers to meet special needs.

**Taking another look at "accountability."** What really counts is not all the "stuff" that makes a school look like a school, but what the school intends as a good education, how far it carries that intention, and to what

---

[10] Monk, D. H., & Haller, E. J. (1986). *Organizational alternatives for small rural schools. Final report to the legislature of the state of New York.* Ithaca, NY: State University of New York. (ERIC Document Reproduction Service No. ED 281 694)
[11] Stephens, E. R. (1991). *A framework for evaluating state policy options for the reorganization of rural, small school districts.* Charleston, WV: Appalachia Educational Laboratory and ERIC Clearinghouse on Rural Education and Small Schools. (ERIC Document Reproduction Service No. ED 332 855)

effect. If a school knows what it and the community want, if that aim is proper and objectively important, and if the school is doing it well and safely, then the community and the state should be pleased. But to whom is the school accountable for such purposes and effects? The state government? Taxpayers in general? The community? Parents? Children? These questions cannot be answered easily, because each audience might ask for different things. Accountability is possible only when those most involved (the vast majority of parents, teachers, administrators, and children in particular local schools) are so involved that they understand what is going on and why.

Site-based decision making, parental involvement, and collaboration with the community are critical elements in accountability, though seldom considered as such. They require long-term nurture and development, and high levels of support if they are to be successful (see Box 2.11).

---

Box 2.11
**Site-Based Decision Making**

Researchers from the Appalachia Educational Laboratory have been studying changes in four rural school districts in Kentucky. New reform legislation passed in 1990 required schools to establish "site-based decision-making councils." Here is what the researchers concluded in 1994:

Some councils in our study, largely through the efforts of key individuals, took advantage of their new authority and the opportunity for input and became important decision makers in their schools. Other councils played only a minor role at their schools. Even where councils exercised considerable authority, however, parents were often left on the fringes of decision making. It appears that some extra effort is required to enlist parent involvement where such involvement is not part of the school's tradition—especially in the current economic climate, in which many parents work outside the home. If parents are to participate fully in SBDM [site-based decision making], educators must learn to share their expertise, and parents must assert their right to the knowledge they need for full participation. Both parties must be willing to expend the time and energy necessary to bring all council members up to the knowledge level needed to make policy decisions about the school.

From: Coe, P., Aagaard, L., Kannapel, P., & Moore, B. (1995). *1993-1994 annual report: AEL's study of KERA implementation in four rural Kentucky school districts.* Charleston, WV: Appalachia Educational Laboratory.

**A final warning.** Influencing policy decisions at the state level is difficult work—one reason lobbyists are paid so well. Few people can deliver the decisions that any particular group might want.

Part of the reason is that policy making is just not a rational process. Both emotionalism and desperation may go into making a policy, though most may argue that decisions based primarily on emotionalism or desperation are bad decisions. Often the public is seen as overly emotional. This chapter, however, has told a story in which policy makers seem to have ignored some very important *facts* and dismissed some very compelling *reasons*.

Policies may even be used to deflect attention from something unpleasant to give the appearance of wise action. Consolidation appears to lend itself well to such misuse—it has mythical qualities (questionable economies of scale, the offer of specialized courses); it promotes the (mis)impression that government is using taxpayers' money more efficiently; and it helps create the impression that government is moving schooling into the future—into the 20th or 21st century, whichever applies! (See Box 2.12.)

In any case, caution is in order. Do not expect that giving good reasons supported with true and accurate evidence will cause your opposition a great deal of grief. These things are important, but they need to be presented powerfully—with the support of friends, neighbors, and allies. Building these alliances and getting them to work well is very important to the success of a grassroots effort; and this observation applies to the local level as well as to the state level.

Rural voices go unheard on the state level because they are few and far between. If you wish to affect state policy, you need to join forces with others around your state. Together you need to define the characteristics of positive rural education policies that you can all promote.

This chapter concludes with a short list of key studies and literature reviews about school size, divided into three groups: (1) curriculum and course offerings, (2) student achievement, and (3) finance and policy. See chapter 6 for brief summaries of the findings reported in some of these studies.

## Bibliography

### Curriculum and Course Offerings

Haller, E., Monk, D., Spotted Bear, A., Griffith, J., & Moss, P. (1990). School size and program comprehensiveness: Evidence from high school and beyond. *Educational Evaluation and Policy Analysis, 12*(2), 109-120.

Holland, A., & Andre, T. (1987). Participation in extracurricular activities in secondary school: What is known, what needs to be known? *Review of Educational Research, 57*(4), 437-466.

---

Box 2.12
**Public Education Bankrupts State!**
**Rural "Primitives" At Fault!**

Alan DeYoung and Craig Howley made the following claim in a 1992 article on the politics of consolidation:

> Citizens seeking pedagogical "facts" supporting rural school consolidation are rarely given any by their local school boards or the state department of education. Upon discovering that the experts have few empirical studies to support claimed school improvements for their districts, these same citizens typically express bafflement, then outrage and determination to "act up." ....An unsympathetic editorial writer in a recent edition of [the state paper], exasperated at the resistance to consolidation exhibited by rural citizens, repeated the key themes of the governor's group:

> I believe that the case for consolidation is overwhelming. Without it [this state] will continue to operate schools too small and too poor to teach classes that are mandatory if our kids are to keep up with the rest of the country....*Consolidation has to come. Otherwise public education will bankrupt the state* [italics added].... Closing a school stirs primitive fears...

From: DeYoung, A. J., & Howley, C. B. (1990, Summer). The political economy of rural school consolidation. *Peabody Journal of Teacher Education, 67*(4), 63-89.

---

Miller, B. (1989). Review of the research on multigrade instruction. In B. Miller, *The multigrade classroom: A resource handbook for small, rural schools,* pp. 4-50. Portland, OR: Northwest Regional Educational Laboratory. (ERIC Document Reproduction Service No. ED 320 719)

Monk, D. (1988). *Disparities in curricular offerings: Issues and policy alternatives for small rural schools.* Charleston, WV: Appalachia Educational Laboratory. (ERIC Document Reproduction Service No. ED 307 096)

Monk, D. (1990, March). *Transcending the effects of school size on the high school curriculum.* Paper presented at the annual meeting of the American Education Finance Association, Las Vegas. (ERIC Document Reproduction Service No. ED 326 370)

Monk, D., Haller, E., & Bail, J.P. (1986). *Secondary school enrollment and curricular comprehensiveness.* Ithaca, NY: Cornell University. (ERIC Document Reproduction Service No. ED 287 628)

## Student Achievement

Barker, R., & Gump, P. (1964). *Big school, small school.* Palo Alto, CA: Stanford University Press.

Fetler, M. (1989). School dropout rates, academic performance, size, and poverty: Correlates of educational reform. *Educational Evaluation and Policy Analysis, 11*(2), 109-116.

Fowler, W. (1992, April). *What do we know about school size? What should we know?* Paper presented at the annual meeting of the American Educational Research Association, San Francisco. (ERIC Document Reproduction Service No. ED 347 675)

Friedkin, N., & Necochea, J. (1988). School system size and performance: A contingency perspective. *Educational Evaluation and Policy Analysis, 10*(3), 237-249.

Haller, E., Monk, D., & Tien, L. (1993). Small schools and higher-order thinking skills. *Journal of Research in Rural Education, 9*(2), 66-73.

Howley, C. (1989). Synthesis of the effects of school and district size: What research says about achievement in small schools and school districts. *Journal of Rural and Small Schools, 4*(1), 2-12.

Huang, G., & Howley, C. (1993). Mitigating disadvantage: Effects of small-scale schooling on students' achievement in Alaska. *Journal of Research in Rural Education, 9*(3), 137-149.

Kleinfeld, J., McDiarmid, G., & Hagstrom, D. (1989). Small local high schools decrease Alaska Native drop-out rates. *Journal of American Indian Education, 28*(3), 24-30.

Pittman, R., & Haughwout, P. (1987). Influence of high school size on dropout rate. *Educational Evaluation and Policy Analysis, 9*(4), 337-43.

Plecki, M. (1991, April). *The relationship between elementary school size and student achievement.* Paper presented at the annual meeting of the American Educational Research Association, Chicago, IL.

Toenjes, L. (1989). *Dropout rates in Texas school districts: Influences of school size and ethnic group.* Austin, TX: Texas Center for Educational Research. (ERIC Document Reproduction Service No. ED 324 783)

Walberg, H. (1989). District size and student learning. *Education and Urban Society, 21*(2), 154-163.

Wihry, D., Coladarci, T., & Meadow, C. (1992). Grade span and eighth-grade academic achievement: Evidence from a predominantly rural state. *Journal of Research in rural Education, 8*(2), 58-70.

## Finance and Policy

Augenblick, J., & Nachtigal, P. (1985, August). *Equity in rural school finance.* Paper presented at the annual meeting of the National Rural Education Association, Kansas City, MO. (ERIC Document Reproduction Service No. ED 258 788)

Bass, G., & Verstegen, D. (1992). Informing policymakers about the impact of state funding formula components on rural schools. *Journal of Research in Rural Education, 8*(1), 15-25.

DeYoung, A., Howley, C., & Theobald, P. (1995). The cultural contradictions of middle schooling for rural community survival. *Journal of Research in Rural Education.*

DeYoung, A., & Howley, C. (1990). The political economy of rural school consolidation. *Peabody Journal of Education, 67*(4), 63-89. [issue actually published in 1992]

Marshall, D. (1988, February). *The cost of small schools.* Paper presented at the annual Canadian National Symposium on Small Schools, Toronto, ON. (ERIC Document Reproduction Service No. ED 310 505)

Rogers, B. (1992). Small is beautiful. In *Source book on school and district size, cost, and quality.* Oak Brook, IL: North Central Regional Educational Laboratory. (ERIC Document Reproduction Service No. ED 361 163)

Sergiovanni, T. (1993, April). *Organizations or communities? Changing the metaphor changes the theory.* Paper presented at the annual meeting of the American Educational Research Association, Atlanta, GA. (ERIC Document Reproduction Service No. ED 376 008)

Stephens, E. (1991). *A framework for evaluating state policy options for the reorganization of rural, small school districts.* Charleston, WV: Appalachia Educational Laboratory and ERIC Clearinghouse on Rural Education and Small Schools. (ERIC Document Reproduction Service No. ED 332 855)

Stern, J. (Ed.). (1994). *The condition of education in rural small schools.* Washington, DC: U.S. Department of Education, Office of Educational Research and Improvement. (ERIC Document Reproduction Service No. ED 371 935)

Walberg, H. (1992). On local control: Is bigger better? In *Source book on school and district size, cost, and quality.* Oak Brook, IL: North Central Regional Educational Laboratory. (ERIC Document Reproduction Service No. ED 361 164)

CHAPTER 3

# What Others Have Done:
# Community as Focus of Study

T his chapter and the next are about a few well-known options that are in successful use in rural schools around the country. In this chapter we focus on (1) using your community as the actual focus of study, (2) the pioneering efforts of the Foxfire program in Georgia, and (3) rural enterprise as a strategy for improving education and community at the same time. In chapter 4, we will explore (1) the 4-day school week as a restructuring tactic particularly suitable for rural schools; (2) the mixed-age classroom, a traditional practice being revisited as a restructuring tactic; and (3) the use of technology for a variety of purposes. There are a great many more options. See chapter 6 for ideas and resources to supplement those considered in chapters 3 and 4. For example, one new publication listed in chapter 6, titled *Pulling Together*, describes 250 resources— products and services—developed especially for rural schools.

The six options considered here and in the next chapter are so widely known and discussed that you will probably want to consider them. They also serve as excellent illustrations of the sorts of things that are possible in small rural schools. They were all developed nearly from scratch by thoughtful people confronting truly difficult issues, with no ready-made solutions in sight.

In fact, ready-made solutions are something of a deception. Education is not like medicine and ignorance is not like a disease: You can't take any educational prescription too literally. Just as there is no optimal size for a school, there can be no predetermined optimal program for a school, nor any ready-made solution for a problem. Problems, like schools, are unique. As you read the three sections of this chapter, keep this fact in mind. We encourage you to use the standard teachers' tactics for building a repertoire of activities and materials: "Beg, borrow, and steal."

## The Community as a Focus of Study

One of the best ways to achieve combined educational and community goals at little cost is to use your own community as your school's focus of study. This can be done in many ways.

In one West Virginia community, kindergarten classes make a number of forays into the community each year. They visit a local dentist's office and ride in his fancy chair. They go to the post office and help put letters in boxes. They go to the sheriff's office and get fingerprinted. They tour the local shoe factory. These five year olds are using their community as a focus of study.

In Moab, Utah, the Outdoor Education Project uses the natural environment of the area as the pivot for the science curriculum. Since the community is located near two national parks, its curriculum also includes courses related to tourism and entrepreneurship. Science and local community and economic development are studies that contribute to one another in Moab. Here, too, the community is a key focus of study.

Ways to use your community as a focus of study run the gamut from kindergarten field trips to full-blown endeavors like the Foxfire program in Rabun, Georgia, or school-based enterprises intended to spin off into independent businesses. Whether you start large or small, any community-based activities you promote will have these benefits in common:

- they will enhance your students' appreciation of their own community;

- they will engage your students in more active, more relevant learning; and,

- handled thoughtfully, they will increase the community's awareness of its young people—their dreams and capabilities.

While some people chase expensive solutions to contemporary educational needs, the greatest resource of all—real life in real communities—is going to waste.

**How it can work.** Some small communities suffer for want of newspaper coverage. Imagine a high-school teacher who is concerned about her students' writing. This teacher does not have any journalism training *per se*, and does not know how to put together a newspaper. But she does know that people in the community would like more coverage of their community than the regional paper provides.

She suggests to her students that they start an area paper. The idea appeals to the students, and together they check out a few library books on news writing. For their first assignment, the students divide up the various tasks—some covering news events, some writing editorials on local issues, and some conducting interviews for possible feature stories. They visit the offices of the regional newspaper to see how it is put together. They invite the paper's editor to their class to explain the flowchart of tasks that make up the production schedule for a small paper—who does what in what order to get the paper out on time. They hold a schoolwide name-the-paper contest, they ask the PTO to front the money for the first edition, they solicit subscriptions: You can make up the rest.

It's true that most such ventures flounder at some point in the process. But what's important is not so much the product that students produce as the experience, thinking, and work that engages them. Even if the paper ceases publication after six months or a year, there are gains for both community, school, and students. The community gets to know its young people better and the school makes clear its commitment to and involvement with the community. But the students learn:

- how to begin something they knew nothing about and how to keep learning as they go along;

- some of the techniques of writing and design associated with publication;

- some of the techniques associated with managing a business; and, just maybe,

- some of the issues involved with a free press: laws, the role of opinion, and how to take as well as give criticism.

How is this venture different from a regular high-school newspaper? In some ways, maybe it's not so different. But it surely carries with it all the weight of a real-life enterprise: It is more visible and it has greater risks (including financial and legal ones).

Using the community as a focus of study is not at all a new idea, but it is one that is seldom used. It takes a lot of work and planning—for making and finding special materials (that is, using something besides a textbook), for going places, and for doing different things.

For some time now, however, educators have talked about "authentic learning," which is a contemporary school-reform idea very much in line with using the community as a focus of instruction. The basic idea is simple: Sitting at desks and doing worksheets or answering questions from the end of the chapter in the textbook is *not* authentic learning. It's phony learning, and we know, in fact, that repetition and drill have distinctly limited value. Over-use is easy in schools as they normally exist; it's the path of least resistance. Authentic learning, however, puts drill in its place and keeps it from becoming "drill-and-kill." Authentic learning involves plenty of discussion, it treats ideas as every bit as important as knowledge and skills, and it involves students in real-life (or lifelike) activities. These are just the sorts of activities required for successfully using the community as a focus of learning.

Like any instruction, however, community-based learning (and other sorts of authentic learning) can be done badly or well. And doing this sort of thing is tricky. The real world doesn't neatly divide itself into school subjects, and any given real-world situation may combine mathematics and social studies, or it may contain things that are normally difficult for children to consider. Handling all this ambiguity is difficult even for a highly experienced teacher (see Box 3.1).

## The Foxfire Approach

The heart of what is called the "Foxfire approach" lies in the long tradition begun by John Dewey. Its methods are child-centered, it features hands-on activities, and it aims to nurture a true education delivered by teachers who think long and hard about what they and their students are doing. All of these features make the approach very much consistent (for the time being, at least!) with the broad intentions of many current reform programs. (See Box 3.2 for an enumeration of Foxfire's "core practices.") Foxfire persists because its core practices contribute to the growth and satisfaction of so many teachers and students nationwide.

---

Box 3.1
**The Community as Diversion: How *not* to**

A grade-school class tours a local factory on a field trip. The teacher does not help the class raise questions or think about the factory before they go. The parts of the factory they visit are so noisy, no one can talk while they are there—a factory employee leads them silently past busy machinery and workers. When they have finished the tour, they get right back on the bus and return to school. At school, they spend 15 minutes that afternoon "debriefing." End of experience. They don't research answers to the questions that cropped up during the debriefing; discuss the factory's role in the local economy; or learn what happens to products made at the factory— who buys them, where they go, and so forth. They don't draw pictures or write stories about the factory. How come? They've got to get on with their social studies workbooks.

If you're looking for a way to make learning authentic, relevant to students' lives, and open to the use of community as a focus of study, the Foxfire approach may be your answer. By using a classroom method that brings the students into a dialogue to determine what they find authentic, then asking them "How?" they want to achieve learning objectives, Foxfire helps teach trust, respect, and project-oriented teamwork through everyday activities.

The Foxfire approach is made up of many things: a truckload of practical wisdom about how to make classrooms work well; a philosophy

---

Box 3.2
**Foxfire's Core Practices**

1. All the work teachers and students do together must flow from student desire, student concerns.

2. Therefore, the role of the teacher must be that of collaborator and team leader and guide rather than boss.

3. The academic integrity of the work must be absolutely clear.

4. The work is characterized by student action, rather than passive receipt of processed information.

5. A constant feature of the process is its emphasis on peer teaching, small group work and teamwork.

6. Connections between classroom work and...the real world outside the classroom are clear.

7. There must be an audience beyond the teacher for student work.

8. As the year progresses, new activities should spiral gracefully out of the old.

9. As teachers, we must acknowledge the worth of aesthetic experience.

10. Reflection—some conscious, thoughtful time to stand apart from the work itself—is an essential activity that must take place at key points throughout the work.

11. The work must include unstintingly honest, ongoing evaluation for skills and content, and changes in student attitude.

From *Hands On: A Journal for Teachers*, issue 50 (Spring 1995), pp. 2-3. Each of these points is elaborated in some detail. (*Hands On* has changed its name to *The Active Learner: A Foxfire Journal for Teachers.*)

about learning and about the intrinsic relationship between schools, communities, and individuals; faith in the teaching profession and what it can accomplish; and a stubborn willingness to take risks, to look continually for more meaningful learning opportunities, and to trust in students' natural abilities.

The Foxfire story is told in detail in *Sometimes a Shining Moment*.[1] Fresh from college in the mid-1960s, Eliot Wigginton began his career teaching English to very reluctant students in a small, very traditional, private school in rural Georgia. His first experiences were disastrous, and Wigginton searched for alternatives to the required lessons on grammar and *Julius Caesar*.

The alternative, at first, was a student literary magazine, which transformed itself rather quickly into a magazine focusing on the rural history of the surrounding community. Students researched traditional subjects and trades, such as hog-butchering, chair-caning, building log houses, and so forth. Many—if not most—of the subjects students researched were cultural practices on the verge of extinction. It was mostly the old people in the community who remembered and could demonstrate the skills to students.

The venture clicked, in more ways than one. Students—previously bored, indifferent, and disruptive—started doing research and writing assignments eagerly. They began to understand how the local knowledge and wisdom that existed in their community contributed to *their* lives, helped make sense of *their* world, and was valuable in its own right. But people in the community were immensely pleased, as well, especially the elders who provided the source material. And when the published work first appeared, the rest of the community became enthusiastic supporters.

*Foxfire Magazine* embarked on a regular publication schedule, with an ever-increasing readership. As the issues and articles accumulated, however, Wigginton worked with an old college friend to bring out the first of nine *Foxfire* books. A tenth volume appeared in 1991, to commemorate the 25th year of this durable experiment. The Foxfire books each went through several printings, with sales in the hundreds of thousands.

The program expanded considerably, partly with the help of the endowment made possible by its astounding early success. Most recently, Foxfire's work has focused on its Teacher Networks, established in many states, to help thoughtful people take on the sorts of active-learning projects that Foxfire has come to exemplify (see Box 3.3).

One thing to keep in mind is that Foxfire is an idea and a program developed in *rural America and exported to urban America*. There are

---

[1] Wigginton, E. (1985). *Sometimes a shining moment: The Foxfire experience.* Garden City, NY: Anchor Press/Doubleday.

## Box 3.3
### Foxfire Kids Speak Up

Children from a third-grade Monongalia County (West Virginia) classroom where Foxfire is alive and well were asked this question: "What is the difference between the Foxfire way of learning and the traditional way of learning?"

**The Foxfire Way:**

It's fun.

Kids want to do it.

We like to find out what it is about and try new things.

Kids get to have responsibility.

Kids get to do more. It's not all listening to the teacher talk and reading out of books.

Kids get to do what they want to do.

We learn our way and get to our goal by learning our way.

We don't just sit in desks, we exercise.

It's more active; we get to draw and color.

Foxfire is like playing outside in summer.

**The Traditional Way:**

It's boring.

Kids don't want to do it.

We don't want to do the work this way; it's stupid work.

You have to just sit and listen to the teacher talk and go blah, blah.

During lectures you have to sit and you can't get a drink because you may miss something the teacher thinks is important.

You get in trouble this way because you may fall asleep.

You have to raise your hand to talk and you never get picked on.

You look at the book and you don't want to do it. The book makes me feel uptight.

From: *Cracklin's*, newsletter of Mountain Fire, the West Virginia Foxfire Teacher Outreach Network.

many Foxfire-type projects in cities. Usually, educational innovations flow the other direction, from urban to rural areas.

Another thing to understand is that the Foxfire books' unique success had a lot to do with interest in the late 1960s and early 1970s in rural living in general. This was the time of the so-called rural renaissance, when urban areas lost population—a lot of it—to rural areas. Throughout the 1970s, people flocked to rural areas, many of them in search of a more essential way of life than they could find in the cities. By the early 1980s, the trend had returned to the familiar pattern, with population leaving rural areas once again. At the same time, interest in new volumes of the *Foxfire* books declined.

The public praise was partly a matter of fortune smiling on a risk-taker working in the right way, with the right students, at the right time. The point is not the glamour of the Foxfire idea—but its potential for helping kids learn better about the world and about themselves. In classrooms across the country, the Foxfire approach is demonstrating its adaptability— from kindergarten to college, in cities, suburbs, and small rural schools. The projects and products of each classroom vary, but the core practices of the method remain constant.

Finally, it is common to find people somewhat confused about the Foxfire approach. On the one hand, there are all the lovely *Foxfire* books about folk culture and old-time lore. On the other hand, the Teacher Networks and the Network magazine, *The Active Learner* (formerly *Hands On*), exhibit very few stories about the old-timey images most people associate with Foxfire. Everyone remembers the commercial successes; but Foxfire's biggest contribution is doubtless the support the Teacher Networks have provided to thousands of teachers to do things differently.

## Schooling and Economic Development

The relationship between schooling and local economic well-being is probably more troublesome in rural areas than in suburban or urban areas. Typically, ambitious, well-educated young people move away from rural to more urbanized places. Thus, it often seems that better schooling only serves to diminish rural communities and their economies.

Clearly, a different sort of schooling might produce a different effect. Instead of breaking the generational circle (as successive waves of younger generations abandon the country for the city), it could strengthen it. It could show young people a way forward in their own communities; it could help reveal to them the idea that the work of preserving and cultivating their own communities is at least as worthy as moving away in pursuit of an exciting cosmopolitan career. And it could help young people assess more clearly the trade-offs that moving away entails. A curriculum that honors community helps, and a classroom method that values student input is also a big boost. A variety of enterprises might make a more explicit connection to local economies, and such options are worth considering. When the local community is a focus for school activities, however, students and teachers can contribute indirectly—and even directly—to improvements in the local economy.

This section of the chapter describes how innovative teachers, administrators, students, and community members have linked learning and business opportunities. These people often begin with a single goal in mind— either a real-life learning project or an economic revitalization effort—but find later that many goals are addressed at once.

Take, for example, the story of Hunters, Washington, originally told in 1990 by Jackie Spears and her team of researchers.[2] The Columbia School District is one of the poorest in the state of Washington. Eighty percent of the students receive free or reduced-price meals at school. The local economy is severely depressed. A number of years ago, the state game department contacted the local school to see if they would be interested in receiving baby pheasants as part of a raise-and-release program.

The local Future Farmers of America (FFA) chapter took on the project with the intention of attracting hunters from the Spokane area. The FFA later took on commercial rainbow trout aquaculture, as well, raising and releasing over 90,000 trout into streams in the area.

How did all of this new wildlife help the community? By helping to boost the hunting and fishing business and giving the students and community a measure of pride.

- The FFA won the state award for "Building Our Community."

- Tourism increased substantially, sparking entrepreneurs to start a new mobile home/RV park and two new gas stations to help serve the influx of hunters and anglers.

- Graduating seniors increasingly decided to continue their schooling and, in the class of 1989, 20 of 23 graduates went on to college; in fact, three of them intended to take up careers in wildlife management.

This story shows that smallness can be an advantage. A routine but thoughtful contact led to unanticipated benefits, just because someone said "yes" at the right moment. Students and teachers got involved and made commitments that they carried through. But, in a more impersonal environ-

---

[2] Spears, J. D., Combs, L. R., & Bailey, G. (1990). *Accommodating change and diversity: Linking rural schools to communities.* Manhattan: Kansas State University, Rural Resource for Education and Development. (ERIC Document Reproduction Service No. ED 328 392)

ment, such developments can more easily encounter a lot of resistance: bureaucracy, apathy, concern over risks. And even if a similar effort succeeded in a city, its small scale could well mean that few people noticed. In a small community, the effects are more likely to be noticed and celebrated.

The biggest spinoffs for students may be the educational ones, in the broadest sense. They learn that they have influence, and they learn that their actions count. Community members may also begin to look on their young people and their school with renewed pride. (Even the athletic teams broke a losing streak in Columbia, Washington, winning three successive championships!)

It's true that such successes cannot be guaranteed; and it's true that such opportunities exist everywhere. But before considering this issue further, let's pause for a quick lesson in rural economics because, in order to consider the topic of schools and rural economics sensibly, we have to get three things clear.

**Quick lesson in rural economics (the bad news).** All over America, rural communities are economically vulnerable; continued existence for many may be in doubt. The reasons are not very difficult to understand.

First, rural economies are generally a lot less diverse than urban economies. This is partly a matter of size. In a small community, one or two employers (for instance, the school and a factory) may employ a large portion or even a majority of workers. Even in large towns (say, with populations of 25,000 and more) it's not uncommon for a single employer to dominate the job scene. Only in larger cities is a diverse economic base more common. And even there, when one industry (say, car manufacturing, as in Detroit) dominates, disaster can strike when industry-wide changes bring on a reversal of fortune.

Second, *rural* means, among other things, out-of-the-way: the backwaters, the hinterlands, the "boonies." Though rural economies are influenced dramatically by national and international developments, the reverse situation—urban areas being affected by developments in rural areas—is very uncommon.

Why? Cities are the economic centers of the world economy. And this helps explain, too, why the practices of urban schooling so commonly get exported to rural areas. Cities have the economic power and, for this reason, the concerns of rural people generally aren't taken into consideration. Rural economies are net exporters to cities; the traditional exports are food, fiber, and minerals, and many rural economies still specialize in producing these things. The U. S. Department of Agriculture actually classifies rural counties on this basis. But, because of industrial improvements (deployed from the cities), fewer and fewer individuals earn their livings from these traditional rural employments. Low-tech manufacturing and service industries (low-paying jobs) have been providing many more of the jobs in rural areas.

Economists call this the *peripheral* (versus the *core*) sector of the economy. Rural areas are, then, peripheral in many ways to the national economy. This does not mean that food, fiber, minerals, and routine manufacturing are not important; imagine what would happen if food, fiber, minerals, and car parts stopped flowing from rural areas into the core industries. The point is that the driving force, the power, of the national economy is located in cities. And that power is so arranged as to provide maximum insurance against the disaster that a complete stoppage of rural exports to the "core" would bring about.

Third, and this is a lot more obvious, the rural population is dwindling. In 1908, 33 percent of Americans lived on farms and 59 percent lived in rural areas. By 1982, only 3 percent of Americans lived on farms, and only 26 percent lived in "nonmetro" areas. And it is important to realize that of this 26 percent, half live in counties adjacent to metro areas. Urbanization means that big cities are getting larger, but it also means that more large towns are becoming cities (a central city of 50,000 is the minimum requirement to be considered a metro area).

**The good news.** It doesn't pay to romanticize or sentimentalize the rural past: It was very difficult, often tragic. The rural standard of living, though not the equal of the suburban, is surely better in general now than during much of the 19th and early 20th century. More important, surveys of rural communities indicate that rural people believe the quality of life in rural areas beats city living hands down.

Still, three facts of rural economic reality—declining population, peripheral economic status, and lack of economic diversity—present a pretty grim picture. But such conditions are a kind of opportunity, too, as the earlier story about Hunters, Washington, implies.

The experience of some communities suggests that a locally focused, school-based curriculum can contribute to serious local revitalization. Similarly, development efforts started outside the school can draw on student energy and talent. Integrating community development and economic revitalization with real-life learning experiences can give rural towns a chance at renewal, while students find meaningful uses for their skills.

**School-based enterprise.** Jonathan Sher's 1977 book, *Rural Education: A Reassessment of the Conventional Wisdom*, did a lot to revive interest in rural schools among a wide audience. Sher didn't just put together a readable and thoughtful volume of what was known about rural education, though. He also made a startling proposal—that rural schools should and could (no one had ever shown it to be possible) serve as a center for economic development in rural communities. Part of Sher's confidence in this proposal definitely had to do with the idea of scale. Schools are an important part of small communities; there is a match between the scale implied by the idea of "community" (where people know each other well and interact often) and the scale of rural schooling. The school is not lost as just one institution among many. Schools and churches, for instance, stand out in rural America.

In the late 1980s, with support from a private foundation, Sher began to put his idea of *school-based enterprises* into action with an organization called REAL Enterprises. REAL stands for "Rural Entrepreneurship through Action Learning."

**Business incubators.** With school-based enterprises, schools serve as business incubators. Business incubators are facilities that offer new small businesses a nurturing environment with shared equipment, reasonable expenses, helpful advice, and access to services and markets usually reserved for more established enterprises. Once a business is on its feet, it moves out from the incubator into the community. The time it takes to move out may vary considerably—from several months to several years—depending on the incubator's policies and the growth rate of the business. Note that business incubators aren't just something for schools; in fact, most incubators are not associated with schools. It's interesting to note that, according to a recent study, small community size is associated with successful business incubation (see Box 3.4 for further details about incubators).

A school building may find the room to house some small businesses, especially if they are started by students. And in many small rural communities, the school may be the only place in town that has simultaneous access to office equipment and light industrial equipment (for instance, for training in wood and metal-working shops and food service facilities). Many rural communities also have vacant public buildings that could use some attention and a facelift, providing an inexpensive home for an incubator.

Certainly, business incubation may seem like a sideline in the overall work of keeping school. But if your community is really dedicated to finding real-life opportunities for students of all ages, small business startups can offer many benefits under one roof.

Successful business startups can offer a lot to a community, but the real point is educational—in just that broader sense considered in chapter 1. Students encounter issues and problems that require all their knowledge, skill, and commitment. This is precisely what a "true education" requires and what is lacking in much schooling. School-based enterprises are just one possible route—but one that has a great deal to do with communities.

**REAL Enterprises.** REAL Enterprises (Rural Entrepreneurship through Action Learning) is probably the best-known and most extensive entrepreneurship program in the schools. Its founder, Jonathan Sher, moreover,

---

Box 3.4
**Business Incubators**

• Business incubators give space, generally under one roof, to a number of fledgling companies (called "tenants").

• Tenants receive services and management assistance from the incubator, usually in exchange for (low) rent, a percentage of sales, royalties, fees, or equity in the company.

• Business incubators are both publicly (49 percent) and privately (12 percent) owned. Community colleges, especially in rural areas, are chief among those who operate incubators.

• Nearly 500 incubators in North America provide assistance to almost 8,000 tenants.

• Of all tenants, 36 percent provide services, 27 percent are involved in technology or R&D products, and 20 percent engage in light manufacturing enterprises.

• Rural incubators account for 28 percent of the total (19 percent are suburban and 53 percent are urban).

• Success rates of tenants are high—about 2 out of 3 firms "graduate" to independent operation.

• Average tenancy inside the incubator for "graduating" firms is two years.

• The National Business Incubation Association provides information and support to interested organizations:

National Business Incubation Association
20 East Circle Drive, Suite 190, Athens, Ohio 45701-3751
voice telephone: (614) 593-4331
FAX:  (614) 593-1996
E-mail:  nbia@info.org  Website: www.nbia.org

---

understands small rural schools from the inside out and back again. Many of his works call on people to give up the idea that bigger is always better and to recognize the real advantages of small schools. His books are an important resource along these lines for anyone considering the range of alternatives to consolidation and school closure. So his insights about school-based enterprise training and good education deserve a close look.

REAL Enterprises is a national nonprofit organization with resources for helping to establish student-owned-and-operated development enterprises nationwide. The program has trained instructors in 17 states and 2 other nations to educate and assist participants at rural high schools and community colleges. As of this writing there are active state REAL organizations in Georgia, North Carolina, Oklahoma, South Dakota, Washington, and West Virginia. The national office is located in North Carolina.

REAL is founded on the belief that changes in the national economy require a cross-section of workers and leaders with the facility to think, not just to follow instructions. For this reason, in the REAL philosophy, students need to become not only good problem-solvers, but good problem-posers and question-askers. This view of what constitutes a good education also has economic implications. The REAL philosophy wants students to develop local economic opportunities and create local jobs—not just to fit into preexisting jobs in urban areas. In the REAL program, rural schools, teachers, and students get the chance to work toward this vision.

The key point to remember is that REAL businesses—as the name suggests—are bona fide ventures that succeed or fail on their own merits. They are not simulations. They are the property and the responsibility of the students who create them. In this way they differ from more familiar programs like Junior Achievement. REAL students create businesses that become part of a community's economic, employment, and cultural base.

REAL uses both classroom and experiential components. The REAL course, which students take for academic credit, includes self-assessment (to set goals and identify marketable skills); community and industry analysis (to determine what businesses are needed and could be sustained by the local economy); business planning (in which each student or business group researches and writes a comprehensive business plan for the chosen enterprise); and, if students choose and are ready to implement the written plan, small business ownership and operation.

REAL projects have a number of educational benefits. Students have access to practical courses—with legitimate academic content and clear relevance to students' lives and futures. Students also learn a lot about the businesses they propose and develop. But maybe the most important lessons have to do with the skills and commitments that students can develop in the process of creating and managing a bona fide enterprise: framing important questions, doing the research to get the answers, making the tough decisions required, and communicating their purposes and aspirations to others. Students who start and manage their own ventures develop the sense that *they can do things*. They learn that things don't just happen to them, but that they have the power to make things happen. Psychologists have a name for this sense of personal competence: *self-efficacy*. Too often, in the model of the school as a factory, students learn just the opposite lesson: That they are blocks of raw material to which things do, indeed, just happen. It's no wonder many adults never achieve this sense of their own power.

**Why enterprise development makes sense in rural economies.** The improved standard of living that characterizes life for many citizens (not all citizens, and fewer in much of rural America than in suburban and urban America) comes at serious cost. Most of the consumer goods come from outside rural communities, including the cars, farm equipment, VCRs and computers, processed food, and refined gasoline or electricity needed to run it all. It's the rare community anywhere that has a car assembly plant in its backyard. Thus, the income of rural communities all around the nation leaks out to the cities that are the hubs of economic life. The trick is to plug the leaks and to make substitutions for the goods that the rural community imports from the urban economy. Many small nations are trying hard to cultivate import substitution. The strategy can work for rural communities in the United States, too.

One of the leaks that can be plugged is energy. No country on earth— with the exception of Canada—consumes as much energy as does the United States. Gasoline, oil, natural gas, and electricity tend to be imports to the rural economy, so conserving energy would save precious dollars, and every dollar saved is available for other uses. Possibly, if there are provisions for import substitution, energy dollars could be spent in the local community, multiplying its effects as it circulates. Conserving energy helps the entire community save money that can potentially stay in town to nurture other projects. The energy conservation business, in fact, is an untapped opportunity in most towns in the United States. Relatively simple in its technology and training requirements, a home energy consulting firm that helps local residents save on their heating and electric bills could figure among student-run businesses.

One possible start-up tactic could be to provide the service at cost to the elderly or those already receiving energy subsidies. Federal and state money might be available for such a project. Indirect benefits to the school are not difficult to imagine in such a venture, either. Rural areas often have a population distribution that is older than it is elsewhere—because young people have for so long abandoned the country for the city. Closer ties to the elderly will probably translate into higher levels of support (as at levy time) for the school.

Saving energy is not exactly the same thing as substituting imports, since money saved might easily be spent on other sorts of imports. And big-ticket imports like cars are not terrific candidates for import substitution. But maybe people have to go outside the community for car repairs, for car parts, or for insurance. These are typical small-town businesses and all are possible candidates for incubation. But—as we all know—rural

---

**Box 3.5**
**Four Strategies of the Rocky Mountain Institute**

(1) Plug the Leaks

Find out where the money is leaving your community. Plug the leaks—make your use of some resources (like energy) more efficient and begin producing at home goods and services that are now imported.

(2) Support Existing Businesses

The biggest share of growth comes from this source. Part of plugging the leaks obviously involves capitalizing on the existing base.

(3) Encourage New Enterprises

Small businesses need help. For instance, micro-loan programs, business incubators, collaboration among agencies and with existing businesses can serve this purpose.

(4) Recruit Compatible New Businesses

In business, as in education, it makes sense for communities to define their commitments. Once a community has defined its leaks and set some priorities for plugging them, it can recruit companies according to a plan that reflects its commitments.

From: Cole, B. A., U. S. Small Business Administration, & Rocky Mountain Institute. (1990). *Business opportunities workbook: A rural revitalization program for community leaders.* Snowmass, CO: Rocky Mountain Institute.

---

transportation is a persistent problem. One possible substitute for cars is a regional rural transportation service. In New York State, the state legislature actually provided support for such a project, using school buses. But many alternatives are possible.

Part of what students do in programs like REAL is scout the local economic landscape for good business niches. A good niche depends on local tastes, needs, and talents. And every enterprise that is locally conceived and locally operated—instead of being part of a national franchise or chain based outside the community—contributes to import substitution. Services, it turns out, are one of the fastest-growing sectors of the rural economy. The franchises typically do not pay well and do not have the commitments to the local area that residents do.

In a sense, developing new businesses is not about "revitalizing" or "rejuvenating" the local economy at all. It may be more like "claiming" it for the first time. When the rural household and farm was the center of economic production, it produced much of what it needed locally. Our "better" standard of living was made possible through an invasion of mass-produced imports from the city economy. The right new businesses can take some of the action away from the city-based enterprises that meet our late 20th-century needs (see Box 3.5 for one view of economic development strategies).

CHAPTER 4

# What Others Have Done: Options for Keeping School

The three options for school improvement considered in this chapter all concern, most particularly, the actual chores of keeping school. All can be viewed, in the jargon of the day, as *restructuring strategies*. That is, they have something to do with the basic approaches to operating a school in ways different from the factory model (but very compatible with rural ways and circumstances).

The 4-day school week has been widely tried in rural areas, with distinct advantage. The mixed-age classroom, once considered a nuisance and an embarrassment to progress, is making a strong comeback in professional thinking. And, of course, recent developments in technology—computers, interactive software programs, advanced telecommunications systems, and the Internet—are getting a lot of attention.

## The 4-Day Week

How can you save money; have longer class periods for special projects and lab classes; and, at the same time, free up time for special events, teacher collaboration and in-service, and community work? Consider moving the school's student schedule to a 4-day week.

The 4-day week has been tried in school districts across the country. Reports of results are generally positive, including significant cost savings, high teacher and public satisfaction, and equal levels of student achievement. Some studies report improved student achievement; achievement

losses are uncommon.  But the districts that choose the 4-day week share a
number of characteristics:

- small size,
- limited resources,
- large geographical area,
- high transportation costs,
- severe climate, and
- high energy costs.

**How does it work?**  The 4-day week lengthens the school day by about
1 hour for 4 days and eliminates attendance on the fifth day.  In this way, the
4-day week can accommodate the same number of hours of instruction as
the traditional 5-day week.  Table 4.1 compares instructional time for a
sample 4-day and 5-day week.

Table 4.1
**Getting a Full Year Out of the 4-Day Week**

A Sample Schedule

Five-Day Program
180 instructional days per year

| Grade level | Minutes per year | Minutes per day |
|---|---|---|
| Kindergarten | 36,000 | 200 |
| Grades 1-3 | 50,400 | 280 |
| Grades 4-8 | 54,000 | 300 |
| Grades 9-12 | 64,800 | 360 |

Four-Day Program
151 instructional days per year

| Grade level | Minutes per year | Minutes per day |
|---|---|---|
| Kindergarten | 36,089 | 239 |
| Grades 1-3 | 50,434 | 334 |
| Grades 4-8 | 54,058 | 358 |
| Grades 9-12 | 64,930 | 430 |

From:  Hill, J.  (1987, October).  *Will a four-day schedule work for you?*
Paper presented at the annual conference of the National Rural Education
Association, Lake Placid, NY.

The 4-day week can reduce expenditures for utilities, transportation, vehicle maintenance, custodial supplies, and substitute teachers. Reported savings on items in the operating budget vary from 5 to 25 percent. Depending on the community's choices, of course, net savings could well be zero—or could even entail increased expenditures. Paul Nachtigal, who has helped rural schools consider their options for many years, makes the following relevant observation:

> If one is concerned about rural school improvement, the question to be asked is "should we continue to spend $10,000+ for busing students to school five days rather than four, or should we reinvest that money to improve the instructional programs which students interact with during the four days that they are in school?"[1]

**Challenges and strategies.** The 4-day school week is such a big change that it requires careful planning and community consideration. Staffing changes obviously require the active participation and collaboration of teachers and administrators. However, since this option has been used for some time in communities around the country, there are enough resources to help you bring up the issue within your community. The same resources can help you plan to put the strategy into action, if it seems suitable.

You need to bring all affected parties, which probably includes everyone in your community, into the planning. The 4-day week offers different advantages to different interest groups, and also raises thorny questions and problems. Think the matter through sensibly. Approach people with sensitivity to the ways they are likely to view the situation. Do your homework so you can answer questions honestly.

In many states, permission for a 4-day week will require a change in state law or administrative regulations. In particular, states that require a certain number of days in the school year present this problem. The laws are based on the assumption (often a requirement) that days be a certain minimum length. The point is to establish the equivalency of somewhat fewer, longer days with the traditional plan. In other states, however, the law specifies only the number of required hours, not days. Your only requirement may be to establish a schedule that meets the hourly quota. In most cases, however, there will probably be some policy waivers, reports, or other procedures. Find out what these might be.

These problems with the bureaucracy raise an important issue. The 4-day week, as Paul Nachtigal implies, should be understood as a strategy for

---

[1] Nachtigal, P. [n.d.] *What's noteworthy on: School improvement and technology, with a special section on rural education.* Aurora, CO: MidContinent Regional Educational Laboratory.

improving education, not saving money. It has the potential to save money, surely. But the real point is to redirect existing resources to better approximate a good education. This is why we note that expenditures could *increase*. This effect is not unlike what happens to consolidated schools (though perhaps in reverse!). When the main point is to improve education, not to save money, the 4-day week becomes—and can be presented as—a strategy to restructure schooling, one particularly suitable to rural areas.

Your local education leaders are your first resource as far as state regulations go. If they are interested in the idea, they will help. Their support is essential and, even if they are cool to the idea, they must be involved from the outset in considering the idea. Teachers and classified staff members (the school support people—bus drivers, cooks, janitors, and aides) often belong to unions. Their interests must be brought into the discussion.

Classified staff may resist the idea—because one of the ways a 4-day week saves money is through reduced expenditures for support functions. The feasibility of a 4-day week may well depend on the cooperation of this influential group. Different segments of the classified group will be affected in varying ways. Classroom aides will be affected like teachers. Secretaries might continue to work a regular week, and the same goes for custodians. Cafeteria services would be reduced by a day—but additional programs might be added or the workday of the staff might be extended. Bus drivers will be most affected. Whatever your situation, remember: The greatest roadblocks to any effort can be those people who feel that they've been excluded and ignored from the start.

Working parents will also be among those concerned about implementation of the 4-day week. A responsive solution can entail the development of plans to provide child care, or to supplement existing provisions in the community. The problem of providing child care could turn into an opportunity for a student enterprise. It's an opportunity that some communities have reportedly turned into a reality. Employers should be engaged in the discussion. The 4-day work week has saved many businesses money and improved employee morale. Coordinating a school change with a change in local industry might offer positive benefits for all parties.

By itself, the 4-day week offers distinct advantages; but the real utility is that it can accommodate a different vision of schooling, including many of the other options discussed in detail in this handbook and described in chapter 6. Both the longer class periods and the noninstructional day lend themselves to activities that draw students out into the community, whether for study or for enterprise development. Furthermore, the self-examination a community must go through while considering the 4-day week is an opportunity to consider other aspects of the district's practice. For example, the community could decide to become more conscientious about staff development and build training opportunities into the 4-day schedule from the beginning.

Perhaps most important of all is the consensus building that a community must go through when making—or just considering—such a change. Many people who have kept their distance from educational decisions are likely to participate in public discussions about something as momentous as revamping the number of days kids go to school. It can be the start of more active participation by the community.

Throughout this section, we have talked about *considering* the 4-day week. We mean just that. The idea can be brought to discussion by a group of concerned people, but commitment to the idea ought to be held in reserve by all parties. The basic question seems to be the one highlighted previously: Is this a route that this school, district, and community can take to achieve a wiser use of resources? Maybe and maybe not. A community needs to ask questions, define some answers, discuss issues, and reach some consensus before the basic question can be answered to anyone's satisfaction. Perhaps the worst approach is to insist from the start that "the 4-day week is the way to go." That approach is grossly out of line with the ideas of chapter 3 (where the community is an integral part of the curriculum). A community that is integral to the curriculum will expect to be integral to how the school is run, to "keeping school," and vice versa.

The 4-day week is a promising option. It's not a requirement!

## Mixed-Age (or Multigrade) Classrooms

Does your school have classrooms with more than one grade level studying together? Do you believe a classroom like that can provide a good education? One mark of a small school is multigrade classrooms—students of more than one grade level studying in the same room with the same teacher.

But even that way of putting the situation is a bit limiting. Do children come already graded? No. The way we know that a child, for instance, is a third-grader is usually *by age*. Kids in the third grade are generally 8 or 9 years old—unless they have been held back or unless they have skipped grades. So it really makes more sense to talk of *mixed-age* classes, so far as the kids themselves are concerned.

It's true that the way most mixed-age classrooms are run is as if they were multigrade classrooms, though. In this common situation, the kids in third grade use the third-grade book; the kids in fourth grade use the fourth-grade book; and the kids in fifth grade use the fifth-grade books. Or that's the way it's supposed to be. The fact of the matter is that some third graders might more appropriately use books written for the average first or fifth grader, and so on with all the "official" grades. Kids learn to read at different times—just as kids learn to walk and talk at different times. Good teachers the world over give students things to do that match their developmental stage, rather than trying to cram all third graders into the third-grade book. Once in a while, someone will insist that all children in the third grade must be working on the same page of the same book at the same time. It's madness, though, because kids, as every parent with more than one knows, differ from one another even in the same family and often in dramatic ways.

Speaking of multigrade classes actually creates a bias against mixed-age groupings. The single-grade classroom is the model: It's the way things are supposed to be. Anything else is an insult to everyone involved (supposedly). A classroom that "has to" serve three grades is a great inconvenience, at least in the factory model of schooling. Kids, like eggs, need to be "graded" for maximum convenience, in this view. Mixed-age rooms are used by teachers as an example of poor working conditions; by administrators as one of the desperate measures that sentimental attachment to small schools imposes; and sometimes by parents to point out that schools are short-changing their children on instructional time. The mixed-age classroom (in its guise as multigrade classroom) becomes everyone's kicking post.

In view of these common opinions, this may come as a surprise: Studies of elementary schooling suggest that students in mixed-age classes perform as well or better than students in conventional, single-grade classrooms (see Box 4.1 for some expert testimony). They perform well on tests for cognitive skills—like reading and writing—and they do even better on tests measuring attitudes toward school, enthusiasm for learning, self-esteem, and so forth.

As Box 4.1 suggests, mixed-age grouping has now been adopted statewide in several places. But even in districts and schools elsewhere, the practice is catching on, particularly at the primary level (that is, what we normally think of as grades K-3). Like the first several years of life, the first several years of a child's school experience are critical. A child who gets off to a good start early in the school experience gets a kind of "insurance policy" on the rest of the school experience. Practically all children start school with the same level of knowledge and enthusiasm. By the end of third grade, though, wide gaps have begun to appear between "successful" and "unsuccessful" students—that is, between eight year olds who are performing and those who have become disheartened. Can an eight year old be disheartened? You bet. Part of the reason is all the sorting that goes on, sorting that is particularly hard on poor kids. Some researchers have even concluded that the point of all the sorting is to *produce* or exaggerate the gaps between the "haves" and "have nots." This may seem like an extreme view, but the weight of evidence has convinced many people that mixed-age grouping is a way around the dilemma.

---

Box 4.1
**Mixed-age Classrooms**

Interest in the potential benefits of mixed-age grouping in pre-schools and the early primary grades has increased steadily in recent years.... Two large-scale mandates to "ungrade" the first years of schooling are receiving a great deal of attention from educators. One is the Kentucky Education Reform Act of 1990 and the other is the provincial mandate of British Columbia in Canada for ungraded classes in the primary years. These initiatives are likely to be followed in several states where similar efforts are under consideration (e.g., Oregon).

Mixed-age grouping can provide older children with the opportunity to be helpful, patient, and tolerant of younger peers' competencies, and thus give them some of the desirable early experiences of being nurturant that underlie parenting and helping others who are different from oneself. Exposure to older children as nurturers provides young recipients with models of behavior they can emulate when they become the older members of a group. Research on cross-age interaction, peer tutoring, and cooperative learning indicates that an age range of greater than one year can provide a level of intellectual stimulation that supports the development of both intellectual and academic competence. This sort of learning environment is also likely to generate greater social benefits than same-age groups, especially for children who are at-risk in particular social development categories.

From: Katz, L. (1992). *Nongraded and mixed-age grouping in early childhood programs* (ERIC Digest). Urbana, IL: ERIC Clearinghouse on Elementary and Early Childhood Education. (ERIC Document Reproduction Service No. ED 351 148)

---

One of the things that mixed-age grouping seems to do is to provide students with a support group—with younger and older kids available to give and receive lots of help from one another. The studies seem to confirm this claim by showing that mixed-age grouping makes happier kids who learn well.

**A brief history.** Before the mid-1800s, the single-grade classroom was unheard of in most parts of this country. Just 75 years ago, 70 percent of all public schools were one-teacher schools! Automobiles were already becoming common sights at that time. The contrast of one-room schools with the power and sophistication of industrial production was not lost on educators. The common opinion at the time was that schools needed to be brought "up" to the standards of industrial production. As we noted in chapter 1, that insight captures the motive for creating the "factory model" of schooling. Schools needed to be bigger, more scientifically organized, and production (that is, instruction) needed to be broken into little bits that could be efficiently conveyed to students.

The single-grade classroom was seen at the time as a form of progress. It was convenient in many ways for teachers and administrators, and it seemed to promise good things for students. And in the growing cities, large schools did begin to emerge in the mid-1800s. Throughout the 1800s and into the present, the number of places with more than 25,000 citizens increased dramatically; and the populations of the largest cities swelled impressively. Immigrants from overseas and an increasing influx of rural residents fueled the industrial revolution in the United States. Schools could hardly escape being part of this history.

Educational administrators in big cities turned to the single-grade class-room as one way to more easily manage the large numbers of children they had to enroll. The techniques used to fashion urban schools—and they were the dominant models for all schools throughout the 20th century—came straight from the factory floor. There was an entire school reform movement organized under the name of *scientific management*. The father of scientific management, Frederick W. Taylor, was an efficiency expert who showed factory owners how to increase profits dramatically by orga-nizing workflow with minimum waste. Taylor paved the way for mass industrial production and for mass schooling.

But critics in the late 19th and early 20th centuries opposed the move to make schools look and work more like factories. They pointed out that it wasn't reasonable to expect all students of the same age level to be at the same stage of development. And they argued that it didn't make much sense to organize instruction on that assumption. The rush to mass produc-tion, to world power, and to a largely urban world drowned out the voices of the critics. But today—in a postindustrial world—people are beginning to examine the alternatives for schooling.

**Making mixed-age classrooms work.** In a nutshell, mixed-age class-rooms seem to work because they encourage teachers to use a variety of instructional methods that are good for learning. In fact, when mixed-age classrooms don't live up to their promise, it's often because teachers haven't gotten the support they need to run their classrooms differently. But many teachers are able to make the transition with moderate assistance. It's not easy, however, no matter what the level of support. It involves a dramatically different way of thinking about school.

The instructional variety that prevails in mixed-age classrooms (where teachers are thinking differently) gives students a greater variety of ways to learn and to demonstrate their learning. Thus, students and teachers are both less likely to fall into the trap of labeling members of the class, expecting certain students to achieve in all areas, and expecting others to achieve in none. This change in perception (a different way of thinking for students!) is key to changes in their motivation and enthusiasm for learning (see Box 4.2).

Kids who learn the lesson that ability determines the degree to which effort will get results and who believe—through repeated examples—that their ability is low, are not going to pay too much attention to school. And really: Why should they? They learned this lesson about their competence at school itself. What they pick up in this way is a deep-seated suspicion that they don't count at school. They might as well not be there, according to this lesson. And the factory model of schooling keeps reinforcing this lesson, so that by the time these kids reach the age of 16, they can't wait to put school behind them. Oddly enough, many kids who leave school for this reason come back later, after life has taught them another lesson.

Good instruction in a mixed-age classroom doesn't just happen. Teachers in these classrooms face special challenges that teachers of single-grade classrooms don't. The mixed-age classroom requires a lot more planning, organizing, and management skill. It also requires the understanding and support of the principal. Because the single-grade classroom has become the norm, colleges and universities have not taught teachers and principals to deal effectively with the mixed-age classroom. Most educators feel unprepared.

Fortunately, teacher skill requirements for the mixed-age classroom have been pretty clearly defined. Teachers in mixed-age classroom have been good inventors. They have devised new techniques, adopted others, and adapted yet others to accommodate wide ranges of student age, social maturity, ability, achievement, and learning styles. As a result, they have developed and written about effective tools and techniques for achieving excellence in the classroom. Chapter 6 describes a number of guides,

---

Box 4.2

**Believing in Oneself:  Effort CAN Improve Your IQ**

Research has shown that students begin their primary grades "believing that their performance and ability are a direct result of their effort.... By the time a student is about in the sixth grade, effort, performance, and ability become reversed.... Ability is viewed as a kind of fixed quantity that determines the degree to which effort can alter performance."

From: Holloway, S. (1988). Concepts of ability and effort in Japan and the United States. *Review of Educational Research, 58*(3), 327-345.

handbooks, and other resources for teachers, principals, and community members. This is a big literature—a lot has been written over the years—and only a small selection appears in chapter 6.

**On taking sacred cows to slaughter.** When you question the conventional wisdom that makes single-grade classrooms the norm, you're taking an educational sacred cow to slaughter. Watch out!

• Assemble your data carefully—read as much as you can; become really familiar with the available resources (see chapter 6).

• Develop practical ideas about how your school and district can learn the skills needed for running effective mixed-age classrooms.

• Consider providing resources to principals or teachers who feel burdened with mixed-age situations, or a group of parents whose school is believed to be inferior because it has mixed-age classrooms.

• Keep in mind the difference between *multigrade* classrooms (several grades with conventional curricula and instructional methods) and effective *mixed-age* classrooms. Mixed-age classrooms are not stopgaps. They break down barriers of grade and age; they present learning and teaching as acts of sharing; and they are inventive, not regimented, places.

• If you don't have any mixed-age classrooms, consider suggesting the idea as a possible innovation. Do some background work and find an adventurous teacher who might want to give it a try. Work through the PTO, a school advisory council or group, and through informal contacts to attract attention.

## Technology for Small Rural Schools

This is a big topic. Big enough, in fact, to deserve its own book—quite a few are listed in chapter 6. What we want to do here is scout the territory so that you can pursue it at greater depth in a way that makes sense in your own situation. But beware: This is a subject where a lot is changing, and fast. Chances are, by the time this book goes to press, new developments will be debuting in public.

**Postindustrial options.** In discussing the mixed-age classroom, we referred to the *postindustrial society*. The electronic revolution is part of the reason—a major reason, in fact—that the idea of the postindustrial society makes some sense. The postindustrial or *information age* (beginning roughly in 1970) may well prove to be as different from the industrial age as the industrial age (1760-1970) was from the age of agriculture (most of recorded history before 1760).

Computers have begun to change the way we do things in basic ways. Jobs are different; how we think about our work changes; how we relate to others—family members, our boss, coworkers—changes; and how we think about our world changes. For instance, there are fewer and fewer jobs for factory workers (robotics and automation displace human workers); electronic- and voice-mail systems mean most workers have a larger number of interactions with customers or coworkers; and families with home computers often find that videogames and on-line interactions become addictive. Debate rages about whether these changes are good or bad. But, all these changes seem to be related to startling shifts in the distribution of power among nations. There *is* something new afoot—again—in the world, and whatever it is, it is reshaping the world we thought we knew. Computers and the various things they do (their *applications*) are in some way central to the changes.

But computers have not yet "revolutionized" schooling, despite decades of promise. Why or even how we should expect them to do this is not entirely certain, either. Part of the uncertainty has to do with views of education that vary. One common view is that education and training are the same thing and have the same purpose: They should prepare people for jobs. Furthermore, such preparation should be cheap, fast, and to the point. One observer claims that "Had the power of educational technology grown at the same pace over the last four decades as the power of computer technology, a high school or college diploma could be 'produced' in less than five minutes for less than five cents."[2]  In this observer's view, government should get out of the business of keeping school, and turn it over to computer companies (or companies with lots of experience in computerized instruction) who could invent *virtual schools*, which children could enter via their computers, to replace the physical schools that now exist.

It does make sense, doesn't it, that some form of schooling will emerge that is more consistent with the "computerizing world"—just as the factory model took over in the "industrializing world." Not only the technology, but the public rhetoric—speeches by politicians and professional leaders and business people—is in place. And the rhetoric shows the same level of dissatisfaction with today's big schools as prevailed at the beginning of the 20th century with the one-room country school.

Schools today, once again, are seen as being too remote from the real world. Using the community as a focus of study responds to this concern well, however. Schools are seen as too regimented; the mixed-age classroom—as we have just seen—can accommodate a more flexible program. And, clearly, the 4-day week could accommodate some experiments with

---

[2] Perelman, L. (1992, December 10). Hyperlearning: Clinton's greatest opportunity for change. *Discovery Institute Inquiry*, pp. 1-12.

Box 4.3
**What ever Happened to Agriculture?**

| Year | Percent of U.S. Population Living on Farms |
|------|--------------------------------------------|
| 1893 | 42 |
| 1908 | 33 |
| 1920 | 30 |
| 1933 | 26 |
| 1940 | 23 |
| 1950 | 12 |
| 1960 | 8 |
| 1972 | 5 |
| 1982 | 3 |

From: *Rural Conditions and Trends.* (1994). Washington, DC: Economic Research Service, U. S. Department of Agriculture.

virtual schooling, where additional, informal instruction might take place using some type of computer technology that reaches students in their homes.

The appropriate use of technology—perhaps including the grand vision of virtual schooling—is consistent with the other ideas featured in this book: the Foxfire Teacher Networks, school-based enterprise development, the 4-day school week, and mixed-age classrooms. These ideas—like virtual schooling—are timely because they respond to the prevalent dissatisfactions.

Can we know what the future will be like? No, of course we cannot. A good guess, though, is that the future will likely resemble the present in many ways. Stories told hundreds and even thousands of years ago still make sense to us. But, based on what we already know, it does seem likely that the need for people to work in factories will decline in the United States rapidly. Whether there will be enough good-paying jobs in the rest of the economy to replace the lost factory jobs is far from clear. High technology has not yet been a boon for rural areas. In fact, one of the biggest growth areas in rural places has been in low-technology service jobs.

But the common expectation is that, for many Americans, the good jobs of the future will have more to do with handling information than with handling materials during the process of manufacturing. It's not that manufacturing will disappear, just as agriculture has not disappeared. It's just that—as in agriculture—far fewer people will be engaged in production (see Box 4.3).

The expectation, then, is that automation (factories making heavy use of robotics) will drastically reduce the number of people needed in manufacturing. Employment is expected to shift (and is already shifting) to services of various sorts, including such functions as processing, sorting, analyzing, and digesting new and quickly changing information. The truth is that no one knows what these sorts of momentous changes are likely to mean in 15 or 20 or 30 years, not to urban America or to rural America. But in the short term, it does seem that electronic resources (technology) can bring things to the rural classroom that were not possible even 10 years ago.

**New tools.** These new tools include such things as satellite and microwave communications systems; the Internet and other global computer networks; microcomputers of all sorts—desktop, laptop, notebook; compact discs; videodiscs; and so forth. In some of these applications, preexisting technologies (microwave towers, satellites, TVs, and telephones) serve as the *infrastructure* on which the newer technologies build.

There is incredible variation—with innovation taking place at a dizzying pace—in the sorts of setups used in schools. Many schools, a sizable minority, have computer labs these days, while an increasing number of schools have added computers to classrooms. Still, we are a long way from having a computer for each student (see Box 4.4 for some indication of the growth of technology in the United States).

New developments, however, are not waiting for the condition of one computer per student to exist before becoming a reality. So what is happening? An important development is *networking*, in which computers are linked together. The networks can be narrow and local, or they can be wide and international.

In a school, for example, all the computers in a lab are networked or connected to a common computer, called a *server*, that is the home base for a variety of software programs: instructional programs, word processing software, encyclopedias, collections of paintings, talking books, libraries of electronic documents, and record-keeping software. This is a *local area network*, or *LAN*.

If the server is linked with, say, the school district office, and through the district office with other schools, then the network would be a *wide area network*, abbreviated as *WAN*.

Now imagine that this sort of school district network was connected to a huge network that hooked up millions of computers around the world, including mainframes and supercomputers at universities, computers with

---

Box 4.4
**The Computer Invasion**

Computers are appearing everywhere. And when they appear, they proliferate. The first table in this box shows the growth in the number of elementary schools with at least one computer. The first table, though, doesn't give you a very good idea about how many children have regular access to a computer. The second table shows the 10-year increase in the proportion of children aged 3-17 who have access to a computer at home. It also shows the dramatic differences that exist between ethnic groups.

Now the press is on to use telecommunications in schools and, in December 1994, 30 percent of our elementary schools had some connection to the Internet. But only 3 percent of the nation's elementary *classrooms* were connected to the Internet.

The ethnic group differences partly relate to differences in average family income. For instance, 75.2 percent of children in families with incomes above $75,000 have access to computers at home, whereas only 5.6 percent of children in families with incomes less than $10,000 have such access. For this latter group of children, school may be the only place to provide such access. Indeed, an additional 37 percent of children in families with incomes less than $10,000 do have access at school.

---

vast databases at government agencies and private companies, and computers with information from a variety of nonprofit organizations. And imagine that there were fairly simple ways to send information to and from all these computers—simple enough for the average person to learn. That's what the *Internet* is—a global network. It's good to remember that networks are webs—their connections go in many directions—and one web can connect with many other webs of all sizes. That's pretty much how the Internet came into being—numerous small webs got hooked together.

As this chapter is being written, the big, global nets are the form of technology that has captured everyone's interest. Internet addresses are appearing on organizational letterheads and on people's business cards. Radio show hosts and government officials invite comment by electronic

### Percentage of Elementary Schools
### With at Least One Computer

| Year | Percent |
|------|---------|
| 1981 | 11.1 |
| 1982 | 20.2 |
| 1983 | 62.4 |
| 1984 | 82.2 |
| 1985 | 91.0 |
| 1986 | 94.9 |
| 1987 | 96.0 |
| 1988 | 96.8 |
| 1989 | 96.8 |
| 1990 | 97.3 |

All data from the National Center for Education Statistics.

### Percentage of 3 to 17 Year Olds
### With Access to a Home Computer

|      | White | Black | Hispanic |
|------|-------|-------|----------|
| 1984 | 17.1  | 6.1   | 4.6      |
| 1989 | 26.7  | 10.6  | 8.4      |
| 1993 | 35.8  | 13.0  | 12.1     |

All data from the U. S. Census Bureau.

mail *(E-mail)*. Advertisers on television have begun to list "Web" addresses. The *World Wide Web*, or *Web* for short, is an easily learned system for accessing the Internet. Some people are predicting the demise of the postal service (prematurely, in all likelihood) as schools, businesses, and even families set up their own *Web sites* or *Home pages* (addresses) on the Internet.

Computer networks bring things together, but not just the same old things; there are new things to be networked:

• electronic versions of classic books from "Project Gutenberg";

• electronic versions of reports, statistical tables, reference works, and magazines;

- the wealth of material on CD-ROM disks (similar to music CDs, but with information recorded instead of music), including U. S. census files, information about school districts, bibliographic databases (in education, psychology, sociology, the humanities, and hundreds of sub-specialties), encyclopedias, and much more;

- artwork from around the world (some museums are coming online and others have produced CD-ROMs or videodiscs);

- On-line Public Access Catalogs (OPACs), which are computerized card catalogs of major libraries from around the world including the Library of Congress;

- discussion groups (called *listservs* on the Internet); and

- archives of public-access software for a wide variety of computers, including database programs, instructional software, word processing programs, speech synthesizing programs, statistical analysis programs, and programs to compute and graph mathematical equations.

Another form of networking, *telecommunications networks*, use computers, satellites, phone lines, and televisions that are wired together, enabling people scattered among different locations (even around the world) to hear and see one another. Telecommunications networks deliver a variety of *distance education* classes (languages, advanced mathematics and science courses, professional development courses, and so forth) and virtual conferences and meetings.

In the midst of all the excitement about networking, however, remember that teaching and learning can be done well without a lot of gadgetry, but with a heavy investment in people—small schools, small classes, excellent teaching, and motivated students. It's probably not wise to ignore technology, though. Most people these days believe that it's important for elementary and secondary students to become very familiar with the things computers do, familiar to the point of using computers easily to do many different sorts of things.

**What should you do?** Whatever ideas and options you consider—either the few featured in this handbook or the many others described in chapter 6—you need to take a careful look at your needs, goals, and available resources (people, expertise, finances). The smaller the project, the less formal and extensive this needs assessment activity has to be. Chapter 6 contains an extended discussion of needs assessment, so be sure to start there.

In nearly all situations, there will be some relevant application of technology to help, simply because new technologies are cropping up in most of what people do. Automobiles may look a lot like they have for decades—but computers are definitely organizing their operation these days, from mixing air and gasoline to transferring power to the wheels. In a 1994 article, *Scientific American* reports that the amount of computer programming present in common manufactured items is doubling every 5 to 10 years.

The enthusiasm with which technology—computers and computer networking—is greeted, however, is something to view with a healthy skepticism. Technology is not the solution for every problem. Moreover, every difficulty in education is *not* a problem. In the very best of classrooms, teaching is still difficult. In the very best of classrooms, there will be serious conflicts and confusing events. Good classrooms will always include diversity and difference. These difficulties—or challenges—come with the turf. Such challenges can be met, but not solved once and for all, because they are recurrent. Deft teachers learn to bring thoughtfulness and cleverness to the classroom in dealing with such challenges. Some people even think that the lessons teachers give in this way are the most important. It would seem that these lessons can help children understand the world better, grasp its meaning more fully. Technology cannot provide this sort of capacity to meet challenges and handle the ongoing dilemmas of classroom life.

But if you want to bring a course in physics to your high school; to find a partner school in another state (or another country) with whom to do projects; students to become proficient library users; or to do a host of other specific things—technology is a reasonable path. If what you want is to improve students' writing, reading, and mathematics skills; or to give students more opportunities to produce "real" products (instead of just completing worksheets) then technology *may* be part of what you need. In this latter case, you will probably want to organize a formal needs assessments. Again, consult chapter 6.

Two of the common hopes expressed by technology advocates—expansion of curriculum offerings (as with distance learning) and cost savings (as with computerized instruction)—still provoke debate. The debates center in part on whether the addition of computerized instruction will really free up teachers, or if it will actually involve *more* of their time for planning. However this debate works out as technologies mature, the need for teacher training will persist. And perhaps we will have to wait for feedback on "virtual schooling" experiments.

**Appropriate uses of technology.** Part of the point of this handbook is that small rural schools don't have to look like large urban schools. Some people, however, insist that good applications of technology require larger schools. To people who think that technology might help small schools overcome the charge that they can't offer a rich curriculum, this view is discouraging.

Just remember that part of the rationale for large schools is that only schools of a certain size can offer a full range of services. The same sort of thinking can apply to technology. A full range of technology probably is possible only in a large school—specialized computer labs, high-powered LANs and WANs, CD-ROM and videodisc libraries, access to the Internet and other global networks, a specialized technology center for teachers, and so forth.

But the question you need to ask is the same as with the curriculum question: Does our school need all this stuff? Why? An appropriate technology is one that meets your needs, not one that conforms to the image of the ideal high-tech suburban school. The chances are that your school does not need all that stuff any more than your high school needs to offer 150 (rather than 50) courses. If your group really decides to consider getting involved with a new educational technology or helping to upgrade existing systems, consider the following tips:

**Recycle.** Try to use the resources your community already has. Chances are, the hardware is not being used as much as it could be. But be careful. Salespeople may tell you that you should forget most of that old stuff you bought before 1988. In some cases, they may be right. You can waste lots of time trying to get older equipment to work with new systems. But if you find that some upgrades are necessary, try to make sure the school system makes good use of the old hardware. Even an "antiquated" computer can serve excellent purposes in helping someone learn to type or learn the basics of word processing, spreadsheets, and database software.

**Plan.** Any new system should be flexible, both in its ability to offer a variety of courses and in its adaptability to changes in your school's needs. If your area is due to get cable TV or fiber optic telephone lines soon, then a satellite dish may not be a very useful long-term purchase. Remember that microcomputers themselves can be used for a very wide range of functions—instructional, communicative, and administrative. For large projects (where the budget is substantial and the technology is complex), your group may well want to involve local expertise in fashioning a multiyear technology plan (see chapter 6).

**Stay on track.** Don't get bogged down in the details when you are considering technology—it's a real danger. Be careful not to spend more time and money developing and fixing your technology than you spend advancing your goals for school and community improvement. Focus on the big and the mid-range issues rather than technical details of hardware and software: What are our goals? What do we need? What is the relevance to the community? Can technology help? How?

Technologies are not ends in themselves—realize that they are tools and use them that way. This is a point that enthusiasts sometimes forget because the tools can be amusing toys.

**Tapping into the community.** If you want to help keep the technology experience as reality-based as other elements in the curriculum, you will need to get out into the community and see what businesses are using in the way of computers, fax machines, computer networking, E-mail, and teleconferencing. Knowing what is out there can give you an idea of where the school can pick up used or donated equipment. Computers depreciate rapidly, and some companies may be in a position to contribute in kind to a well-conceived project. In fact, conducting such a community survey is a logical project for students. The students get to see what sorts of equipment are being used in real-life situations.

Community members may also be a source of knowledge and skills. Most communities, in fact, have a few informal technical experts who would like to be involved in a project to help the local school. Bank employees, TV service people, insurance agents, extension agents, hospital administrators, health department employees, retailers—many could have knowledge and experience that reaches the level of expertise. These folks can, at a minimum, be involved as coaches. They can meet with school personnel to discuss what sorts of services and support are available locally.

These sorts of initiatives can also serve as the basis for communitywide collaboration. A small community or several small communities can band together to maximize the benefits of establishing and using distance learning, teleconferencing, and global network connections. The same equipment, and perhaps the same services, can be useful to a whole range of community organizations, both public and private. Not only can such collaboration produce reduced capital and operating costs for each involved organization, but it can ensure an adequate level of use to make it worthwhile. Underuse is actually a common problem when technology is introduced, particularly if the planning and purchasing is imposed bureaucratically. Computers can sit unused for months, or even unused entirely, and the reason is lack of a sense of ownership or enthusiasm. Uninvolved parties are reluctant to commit to a project just on the basis of say-so. When many organizations are collaborating, they can support each other in efforts to get trained and use the new technology.

CHAPTER 5

# Doing It Yourself:
# Helping Things to Change

R eaders of this handbook will, we know, approach the activity of school improvement from a lot of different perspectives. There can be sharp disagreements—legitimate differences—over many of the points considered so far. People who have been involved with efforts to make schools better will recognize this fact. Some of the differences involve personal commitments; for instance, a person's vision for education might stress knowledge and skills over understanding, or vice versa. Some people would give priority to self-esteem and others to academic achievement. When these contests erupt into a seemingly unrelated debate, differences in commitments can sabotage a project.

Differences can be aired, of course, and there are good tools for resolving conflicts productively. But working together on a project inevitably involves give-and-take on everyone's part. Not only that, but the interchange has to be a learning experience in itself. Beneath the idea of using the community as a focus of study lies this concept: The relationship between school and community flows in both directions, each learning about the other. This is also the way coalitions form: Participants learn about one another and define their common interests.

## Getting Organized

Whether you are a member of a faculty governing group, a school improvement council that includes community members, a principal or teacher who wants to involve the community, or simply a concerned individual interested in education, you will probably have to do some coalition building. In fact, successful politicians know that whenever concerted action is required, coalitions must be built. And most of all, this means informal contact. In urban areas, this sort of thing can be much more difficult for community members than it is in rural areas: "You can't fight city hall." The closer personal ties and the webs of friendship and kinship that are so common in rural areas make informal contacts easier. But it may also mean that greater tact and better manners are needed to keep things focused and to minimize the threats that offhanded remarks can pose.

So coalition building is a largely informal process, and it's needed for developing practically all projects. There are two basic ways to go about it. You can begin with a friend or an ally with whom you share many commitments. Or you can begin with many people who just happen to have one thing in common. The process in each case, however, aims at the same result—somewhere in the middle (between two good friends and a group of acquaintances or strangers with strong feelings about one issue) is a sizable group of people who can speak with one voice and who hold a number of common commitments. Defining those common commitments, agreeing on them, and articulating them with a common voice is the work of coalition building. Once the coalition is set, it is ready to propose official action, or at least to advocate its commitments in an official forum.

The key is to work deliberately. Take time with each person or level of people (for instance, representatives of the school, community, district, region, or state). Explore with them how their interests might coincide with your commitments (see Box 5.1).

And keep an open mind about your own interests: How do your interests coincide with their commitments? Is there room for concerted action? Can room be made for such action?

Try to discover what methods might work best for all of you. The long-term benefits of this approach can hardly be overestimated. More people = more perspectives = more ideas. And, eventually, interchange and agreement will increase the coalition's power. Also, when the conversation is open, frank, and well-mannered—even when there are disagreements—almost no one feels that something has been forced on them without regard for their concerns. See chapter 6 for more information on coalition building.

**Where to start.** Start small (with a friend) or large (with a group and a single common interest), depending on your temperament, your community standing, and who your logical allies are. If you are inexperienced or just very busy, you may want to start small, with a project that can be readily completed and has popular appeal. Make sure that word about what you are doing gets out, and you will probably find that your action inspires others. If they take on a few projects, you may well have the basis for building some sort of coalition.

Box 5.1
**Interests as the Basis of Need**

Chapter 6 contains a special section on *needs assessment*. Needs assessments are important parts of proposals. They assure the funding agency that (1) the proposal meets the agency's needs and (2) evidence exists that the project is important locally.

But what is a *need*, really? It is the lack of something important. One formal needs assessment technique describes "need" as the difference between the way things are now and the way people—the group being assessed—would like them to be. Needs represent desires or, more particularly, a group's hopes in a given context.

Often, people will desire a stronger, more challenging education for their children, and leap from that desire straight to consolidation as the best method for realizing their dream. They will then view their school's problem as "lack of size," although in reality, the problem may be "lack of quality" or "lack of fit" to local needs. Such confusion of needs and prescriptions (for improvement) can break down the process of building coalitions to improve schools.

You can see why insisting that rural schools become larger can actually be a pitfall: There is no guarantee that larger size has anything to do with meeting local needs. Surely, the longstanding popular outcry over rural school closings is strong evidence that consolidation has generally *ignored* local needs.

If you command significant attention within your community (either as an individual or as part of the group with which you are working), or if you hold a position of leadership (civic leader, bank president, principal, superintendent, president of the teachers organization), you may decide to take action on a larger scale. There are many resources to help you organize an entire community or conduct comprehensive planning within a system—your district, community, or even state (see chapter 6 for ideas).

Starting big has its problems, though. The danger inherent in *comprehensive* or *strategic* planning efforts is that people will feel over-controlled by the process or left out altogether. A delicate touch, honesty, openness to everyone's contributions, and dedication to including the "invisible" members of your community are absolutely essential. A hidden agenda is anathema to large-scale efforts. This problem is by no means uncommon with large-scale projects, so either (1) don't support such efforts or (2) take measures to eliminate the problems.

You may be most effective in the long run if you work on several levels at once. Start a small project to build a track record and use that success to organize a bigger effort.

Or, start at both levels at the same time, giving a lot of time to the big effort, but taking satisfaction from the more immediate success of the smaller undertakings. This is a good way to engage people of differing talents and temperaments. The "doers" will want to get started on something immediately, while your "people people" begin a wider-based organizing process. You may have volunteers who can commit to a small project and a civic leader or superintendent who can coordinate an extensive community process.

Whatever your own opinion on particular issues, you will serve your school and your community best when you work toward agreement about what matters and about what solutions are best. From our own experience we offer, in Box 5.2, a few tips on getting started in the work of coalition building.

## Gathering Information from People

Whatever action makes sense to you, you need to approach it as fully prepared as you can be. Some of the most important information you need is information about and from your local community. Part of this information consists of the sort of things described in chapter 6's discussion of needs assessment. But other kinds of information are important too: community resource lists, records of informal conversations during coalition-building activities, and other information about virtually any—and all—features of life in your community.

Aside from community members and groups themselves, people who can serve as sources of information (up to the state level) include (1) your school district's leadership (don't overlook teachers!), (2) the public relations office of your state board of education or state department of education, (3) the legal advisor to the state board or state department of education, (4) legislative aides for the education committees, (5) your state supreme court librarian, (6) professors—particularly in college and university education programs, (7) state-level staff members of teacher and service-personnel unions, and (8) the education aide(s) in your governor's office.

In your conversations with anyone, be sure to keep a record of the names of people you talk with, just as book authors list their sources of information in footnotes or bibliographies. Moreover, if you read something in a newspaper or popular magazine, the paper or magazine will be able to put you in touch with the author. Most people you contact will be able to recommend friends and colleagues who can provide new information or

Box 5.2
**Getting Started with Coalition Building**

1. Find kindred spirits: others with similar commitments, people who share your concern and can work with you.

2. Gather information about (1) the issues, (2) the research, and (3) other people's ideas, deeds, and plans.

3. Use the resources in this handbook to assess needs, fashion goals, and develop action plans.

4. Build the commitments of interested groups. Find out ways to meet several of their needs simultaneously and get their contributions. Doing this is a source of power.

5. Intervene and solve problems at the lowest possible level. This is where the problems actually exist. It's not as easy as it may sound.

6. Fight only at the highest possible level. A corollary: Involve as many levels as possible in your planning. People tend to identify the "top dog" as the enemy, the source of the blockage. This tendency can get in the way of coalition building; where feasible, involve the "top dog" early on.

7. Develop widespread public discussion: letters to the editor, presentations and discussions at meetings, public panels and debates, and study groups.

8. If you are able to do these things, the next steps will become clearer—for instance, working public consensus into school board decisions or school improvement councils, organizing for political action, or forming a local foundation or support group.

9. And finally, *always be civil.* Good manners help people work out their differences rationally. There is a place for impassioned testimony, but always control your anger and use its energy wisely.

contrasting viewpoints to consider. When you stop getting new names in this way, you know that you have probably identified the key people who can provide information.

## Confronting the Professional Research Literature

Educational information is not terribly difficult to come by. You need to know where to find it, use tools that will get just what you need, and possibly develop some skills in interpreting the educational jargon. Educational research varies in quality and readability. The range is considerable, but the test of quality is NOT whether the conclusions support your position. A good research study could well come to a conclusion that contradicts your position. The real difficulty of reading the research literature—for anyone, including researchers—is making sense of it as a whole. Understanding a single study or a couple of related studies is not usually enough.

So one of the best alternatives is to read a kind of research study called a *literature review*. Literature reviews try to help people—including ordinary citizens, teachers, and others whose forte isn't research methodology—understand what a group of studies concludes. Usually there are some conclusions, but they may be tentative. Other issues may be unresolved, may not be addressed by very good studies, or may have escaped attention.

Some of the best literature reviews are those published in *peer-reviewed professional journals.* These are periodicals (like magazines) to which scholars submit articles that are then reviewed by expert members of an editorial board. Editorial board reviewers read the manuscripts and make suggestions (many manuscripts get rejected). Articles that survive this process get published. Many other good literature reviews appear in books, conference papers, and so on. Chapter 6 lists some of the best literature reviews on school size and rural education. But there are many more topics that you may need to learn about.

**Learn to use ERIC.** The previous chapter talked about the information age and mentioned electronic databases. The ERIC (Educational Resources Information Center) system maintains one of the largest and most-used electronic databases in the world, and it's all about education.

The ERIC database describes nearly a million articles, books, reports, and other information about education and schooling. Moreover, the ERIC system is one of the most accessible educational services in the world. You can, for instance, use its resources by:

• calling one of several toll-free telephone numbers;

• visiting a college or university library, public library, or, sometimes, even school and district office resource collections; or

• computer, via the Internet and commercial global computer networks (for example, America Online).

ERIC builds its database through the work of 16 clearinghouses, which gather documents and articles in particular specialty areas. One of the 16 clearinghouses is the ERIC Clearinghouse on Rural Education and Small Schools, located at the Appalachia Educational Laboratory in Charleston, West Virginia. You can reach their staff by calling 800/624-9120 and asking for "ERIC User Services." The staff will talk to you and conduct a free search of the database.

But you can also ask questions on the Internet. The ERIC system sponsors a personalized question-answering service called *AskERIC*. Just send your e-mail message to *askeric@ericir.syr.edu*. Remember, at least as this text went to press, you can send an e-mail message to AskERIC from all the major commercial networks (such as America Online, Delphi, and Prodigy).

One of the virtues of the ERIC database is that it has a complete indexing and cataloging system—which means, for example, that you can identify literature reviews with great accuracy. It's a lot easier than looking through a library's journals hoping to find what you need.

Aside from literature reviews, you need to know about ERIC Digests. Digests are like literature reviews, but they are just two pages long and are prepared especially for a varied audience. Over 1,000 Digests on a broad range of education topics have been written by the various clearinghouses since the early 1980s. Short, to the point, and of excellent quality, the Digests are available in electronic format. For more complete information about the ERIC system, just call 800/LET-ERIC. Ask for the free guide-book, *All About ERIC*.

The ERIC system is itself part of a larger federal *research and development* (R&D) system, which includes national research centers at over 25 universities; 10 regional educational laboratories (like the one where the ERIC Clearinghouse on Rural Education and Small Schools is located); and the National Center for Education Statistics, located at the U. S. Department of Education in Washington, DC. All of these institutions can be wonderful sources of information. Consult chapter 6 for more information about the federal R&D system in education, with an emphasis on the 16 ERIC clearinghouses and the 10 regional educational laboratories.

## Understanding Who Is Responsible for What

We've developed this handbook for community members as well as educators, but community members are at something of a disadvantage. Educators probably understand who's responsible for what in the community better than people in the community understand who's responsible for what in the schools. So we want to provide an overview of the various educational *role groups*, especially for readers who aren't educators.

The array of players in our public school system, however, is mind-boggling even to those who work in it. Not only that, but every state is different from every other state. In all states, though, the power of state government is so influential that most people have trouble believing that things can be and are different in other states (and even other school districts). This observation applies to educators as well as community members. When you start to think statewide and nationwide, it's necessary to overcome this natural limitation in perspective. Don't assume that the way things are in your state is the way it is everywhere else.

In some states, state government provides most of the money for running schools (the typical situation in the South); in other places (like the Northeast) the bulk of school funds comes from local governments. In some states, schools are dependent on governmental bodies for funding; in other places, schools can levy taxes all by themselves. In some states, districts are organized as county units; in other states, all the districts are town or township districts; and in still other states there is a combination of county and independent districts. In some states, all districts have high schools; in others, high schools may be separate districts entirely; and in still others, an elementary district may send its students to different high schools on a contractual, tuition basis. You get the idea: Your basic assumptions about what schooling looks like generally, based on your experience in a single state, are probably inaccurate. The United States has a very decentralized public system compared to many other nations, both in the industrial countries and in the third world. No wonder there is a great deal of variety.

There are resources that describe this variety in some detail. But what you really need to learn are the details of the structure in your own state. Just remember that comparisons with other states can prove useful. In fact, when state legislatures—which have substantial power over schooling in all states—take on big reforms, one of the first things they do is study what other states are doing. The Education Commission of the States (see chapter 6) is one of the best sources of information for comparing the various states.

Though the balance of power among them will vary from place to place (and not just by state), you will find the following players on every field. Be aware that, as we noted in chapter 3, the various role groups often have different interests. Educators seldom speak with a single voice, and the dominant teachers' organization can often wield considerable power among legislators—as can administrator groups. It is not uncommon for these groups to have quite different agendas, though teacher organizations as a statewide body seldom oppose consolidation schemes developed at the state level.

**Administrators.** This group includes principals, district superinten-dents, regional officers, state superintendents, and their helpers. Administrators generally do not interact directly with students, although in small elementary schools the principal might also teach. Administrators are responsible for making the system work. They interpret policy and see that policy decisions are turned into working programs.

Theoretically, administrators don't make policy—school boards do. But local boards and other policy making bodies (the state board, state department of education, legislators, and governor's office) lean heavily on administrators for information and advice. Administrators are generally in a better position than other professionals to select information and to prioritize issues for policy makers. And they do these things, naturally enough, according to their view of what is important (just as anyone would). Administrators, in short, even as individuals, can exert a strong influence on policy.

Of course, administrators also have their own decision-making authority for a variety of day-to-day issues related to their jobs. And they have the authority of job status. They are generally less well-organized for formal political action than are teachers, so their power based on sheer numerical strength is less. But administrators—no doubt about it—can accomplish a lot with informal networks. The state superintendent, for instance, most often comes to the job with considerable experience as a local or regional school administrator. And the state superintendent and staff exert a lot of influence with the legislature and the state board.

Administrators have significant personal power, for better and for worse. An enthusiastic, sympathetic, thoughtful administrator can establish a positive, caring climate throughout a district. Such a person can involve everyone in decision making and accomplish a great deal through leadership. Being an administrator is a tough job, though, and true leadership—like a true education—is a continual challenge. It is in short supply almost everywhere. That's part of the reason communities need to be involved: They can increase the supply of talent from which true leadership might emerge.

But the importance of administrators is why one major movement in school reform, the effective schools movement, concentrates heavily on developing leadership skills. A terrific school principal can dramatically change what happens in a school. Among educators, it's common knowledge: To make a bad school better, change the principal for the better.

Remember that administrators are in a position to control information. This control potentially affects anything you, as a community member, might try to do. On the one hand, you will need information that only administrators can provide. On the other hand, if you have information that could affect decision making, you will have to present it convincingly to administrators who are in a position to pass it along, use it, contradict it, or bury it.

**Teachers.** As lone voices, teachers often view themselves—with considerable justification—as victims of a bureaucratized system in which every decision is already made. Some believe that their every waking moment is controlled. And teachers often feel that they don't get the support they need from anyone. In many systems, they are right. The larger the system, the more difficult the circumstance of teachers may be, though not every small system is better in this way than every large system. There are good and bad systems in all sizes. As those closest to children's lives and minds, however, teachers and parents are natural allies. In some systems, teachers enjoy strong respect and influence.

In recent years, teachers have organized themselves politically. Because of their vast numbers (over 2.5 million teachers work in the public schools) teachers' professional organizations have achieved significant political power. They affect decision making primarily through collective bargaining (in many but not all states) and through the political influence of their organization at the state level.

As a result of organized efforts and new thinking among school reformers, teachers have begun to acquire substantial decision making authority. They are commonly included in significant numbers in school improvement teams of various sorts. These teams may be called *site-based management teams, local school improvement councils,* or *faculty senates*; some of these groups may include parent or community representatives as well. Whatever they are called, these bodies are getting an increasing say in decisions about curriculum, textbook selection, discipline policies, and hiring in local schools. In some cases, these bodies even exercise control over the school budget. All of these decisions, or most of them, used to be handed down from the district office or from the principal. In some places, school boards find the new powers and actions of these groups a threat.

Unfortunately, relationships between teachers and parents can sometimes be poor, even in small rural communities. Teachers in such cases feel that parents no longer back them up (as they are presumed to have at one time in the distant past). Common complaints are that parents no longer teach good manners and discipline or make sure their kids get enough good food and rest.

Parents can sometimes view both the school and the teachers as threatening their dignity and their control over their children's lives. They may think that teaching is an easy job, or at least a good job—one to be envied. Teaching jobs often *are* among the best jobs a rural community has to offer. But the truth is that teaching is a difficult job, and the responsibilities are relentless. Parents are often so busy with multiple jobs and responsibilities that staying in touch with teachers is very difficult. There are a couple of points to bear in mind.

First, everybody should understand that the good old days were not all they were cracked up to be. Kids did go hungry, discipline was a problem in many rural schools, attendance was often poor, and teacher turnover was high. Much education, as we reported earlier, went on outside the confines of the school—and the common aspiration was to complete elementary school, an aspiration that many people in rural areas fell short of. There was not much room in many schools for understanding or skill development; there was, instead, recitation and rote memorization.

Second, *parents* are teachers, and most *teachers* are parents. Basically both groups are in the same boat: too much to do, too little time to do it, and too many hats to wear. Both groups confront the same world where things are organized too tightly, there is not enough contact among neighbors, and the true and the good too often get lost in the shuffle.

None of this is to deny that some teachers are harmful to students and that some parents are harmful to their children. But there is more common ground between teachers and parents than most of us realize. The common ground should be better cultivated by both sides. As with coalition building, good manners are important. The parent-teacher link is both an issue in itself and a vehicle for accomplishing your goals. You won't get far without teachers, and they will get further with your help than they typically do without it.

**Local school boards.** Though some boards are appointed, most are composed of elected citizens. Sometimes retired educators serve on boards, but, for the most part, board members have little or no experience with educational institutions—beyond having attended them. As a consequence, board members tend to be heavily dependent on administrators, both for information and for guidance. Furthermore, though boards are responsible for a number of financial decisions, most of the money they "control" is tied up in personnel costs. And much of the remainder is committed by federal and state laws and regulations to certain purposes. A local school board's financial ability to undertake new initiatives is very limited. Even so, elected local boards tend to be more responsive to local issues and needs than state policy-making bodies.

If your school board members are elected, they are susceptible to the opinions of voters. At best, they have good relationships within the community and are responsive to citizen activity. In this case, they can help you tremendously, and everybody wins. If not, you at least have the option of organizing voting campaigns to replace them. Indeed, school districts go through some pretty amazing changes when the balance of power on boards undergoes a major shift as a result of elections. In rural areas, for instance, anticonsolidation candidates can sweep into office (usually on the heels of school closures) and even undo previous decisions. But the real test of a board member comes after the election. A board member may come into office as the result of a single-issue campaign, but to carry out the job well, he or she has got to understand all of the issues that come before the board.

In all your dealings with school board members, consider what they really can do, and what they can't. Also remember that they must make decisions for *all* the people. If you are part of an "out group," you can still insist that your needs be considered. But if you are part of a dominant group, make sure you are leaving room for everyone's concerns to be heard. When the board members feel that you are informed and are trying to make things better for everyone, they are more likely to work with you and try to accommodate your interests.

**State school boards.** These bodies fill a policy-making role similar to that of local boards, but for the entire state. In some states they are elected, but they are often appointed. Like local boards, most members are not professional educators, but—because of their visibility at the state level—they are often very educated, prominent citizens. Most of the time they are not heavily involved in the drafting of policies—a job usually done by administrators. Most state board meetings last several days, with lengthy agendas concerning weighty matters of statewide import. Many items are dealt with in a cursory fashion, but the meetings are open to the public, and educators and their organizations commonly present to the state board their views of propositions that they find troublesome.

As with local boards, the commitments of members will vary according to whether they are appointed or elected. Citizen groups often overlook the state board, partly because of its remoteness at the state level, partly because its prominence and close relationship to state government may be intimidating, and partly because its functions may seem more ceremonial than functional. But the state board IS the organization that actually sets policy for the entire state, and the ultimate responsibility for and power over schooling in the United States, as we noted previously, rests within state governments. State boards may not often develop the policies they adopt (which are commonly prepared by the state department of education, in the executive branch of government), but they do have the unquestioned power to reject them, to ask for alternatives, and to revise them.

Remember that the state board's primary source of information is officials of the state department of education, whose stake in the system of schooling is very different from that of parents, citizens, and educators in local communities. Coalitions with the state department and state board, of course, are advantageous—but they are usually founded on relationships cultivated over quite some time.

**Chief state school officer (CSSO).** This person is the chief executive officer of a state's public school system. Like the local superintendency, the position is sometimes filled by appointment and sometimes by election. Appointments may be by the governor in some states, or by the state board in others. The title of this office varies—Superintendent of Public Instruction and Superintendent of Schools are common. The CSSO works in relationship to the state board of education somewhat the way your local superintendent works in relationship to your local board. The CSSO answers formally to the state board, implementing the policies it adopts and directing the far-flung activities of the state department of education. And like the local superintendent, the CSSO exercises considerable authority simply through the routine control of a large portion of the information on which the state board bases its decisions.

The CSSO is certainly a good person to know and have on your side— but reaching this person will prove difficult most of the time. Like anyone on the state level, the CSSO is responsible for a large operation that is not readily responsive to local perspectives. CSSOs typically deal with the larger picture—the smaller, local pictures averaged at the state level. For instance, the average number of students per teacher (student-teacher ratio) for the state may come out to 15 to 1. Your school, though, may have a very different average, and that average itself doesn't show the variation among classrooms in your school. The CSSO will try to base decisions on the big picture—the biggest picture, some sort of average of "what is best" for the state as a whole.

This is a difficult task; maybe an impossible one—but its essence is some form of compromise. That's what an average is—a compromise that gives a single number in place of (possibly tremendous) variation. So what is judged to be the best is a matter of compromise—of negotiation. The challenge for small rural schools is to become part of that negotiation and part of that compromise. That's one of the things that coalition-building can make possible.

Remember, too, that the CSSO—in the midst of all this compromising and negotiating—has to answer to many pressures and taskmasters: limited budgets, a variety of interest groups (not just yours), the legislature, the state board, the governor. The list is long. But you don't get to be the CSSO without having your own agenda. CSSOs are generally smart, clever, tough, and dedicated—they know the ropes.

**The courts.** You may not think of the courts as key actors in the educational system, but they are. School law—the acts passed by the state legislatures and the federal government—is a complex matter. This is not just because there are a lot of laws about a lot of things (some very important and some not so important), but because of the decentralized, state-based system of schooling in the United States. There are important jurisdictional issues to be sorted out: What things do parents have authority over?  What things do teachers have authority over?  What about principals?  What can the local board properly do?  How about the state board, superintendent, and legislature?  Where does federal authority come into the picture?  And then there are key substantive issues to consider:  for instance, the authority to open and close schools; the fairness of state funding systems; the rights of teacher and student; the freedom of religion; and the responsibility to minorities, women, and persons with disabilities.

The courts are there to sort these things out when individuals and institutions cannot agree.  They can enter the decision-making arena only when someone affected turns to them to resolve differences.  Courts are generally reluctant to get involved in matters that they have previously said (in rulings on cases that have come before them in the past) are the responsibility of one administrative authority or another.  But when issues of justice (including civil and criminal issues) are involved, the courts will intervene.

Using the legal system to achieve a goal is expensive and it takes a lot of time.  Clearly, it requires that you (via your attorney) assess the legal arguments available.  Professional help is essential in the later stages, but, once again, you can examine the professional literature to make an initial assessment on your own.  And, for the more ambitious, the state supreme court library is a good place to take a look at the cases that have been decided relevant to your issue of concern.  The training of administrators often includes a course on school law, and they may be able to give you some tips on using the law library.  The literature on the law is a matter of public record, so you do have access to it.  But actual legal action without a lawyer is unwise.

So this route is expensive.  You will, in all likelihood, have to organize a broad base of support to help cover costs—if your case has merit.  And even if the decision goes your way, you may never see the results!  They have to filter through the legal, administrative, and maybe even the legislative systems, and resistance can persist at every turn.  If you feel, finally, that you've done everything else possible, and if you do have a reasonable case, then a lawsuit may be appropriate.  It can—and has—forced bureaucrats and politicians to face issues they would rather avoid.  In making such a decision, have a very clear picture of your needs and interests.  What's lacking?  What are you in the middle of—a big issue of principle or a middle-range practical issue?  Remember that litigation is a tough way to solve a problem that is mainly practical.

**Legislators.**  Because education is a state, and not a national, function, state legislatures actually exercise the highest level of authority over schooling.  They make the laws that govern schools, whereas the state department issues regulations that enforce both acts of the legislature (laws) and the policies adopted by the state board.

This is an important distinction—the one between laws, policies, and regulations. Why? Because attempts to create or change legislation are even more complex an arena than administrative decision making. Like the courts, legislatures must sort out many issues; like the CSSO, they try to figure out a meaningful average; and like state and local school boards, their educational expertise is limited. But because they sit at the top of the chain of authority, there are fewer restrictions—and fewer guidelines—to contain, channel, and structure their actions. What this means, of course, is that legislators have many people making suggestions and trying to exercise influence over them. Many bills get introduced during a legislative session, but few of them—a small minority—actually make it all the way through the complex adoption process. And, if there is much controversy at all, the final act may be quite different from the bill originally put forward.

Laws are hard to change, in particular, once they are in place. For example, if your state has a *law* (that is, an official act of the legislature, rather than an administrative regulation issued by the state department of education) about how many days students must attend school, it will be a lot more difficult for you to get permission to try a 4-day week than it would otherwise. Regulations can be changed more easily. In the case of a law, you have to convince a lot more people who have an interest that is being well served by the existing law, and whose interests may be difficult to reconcile with your interest. Funding of a program, for instance, might depend on the average number of days students attend school. People with a stake in that program might really not object to your experiment with a 4-day week, but changing the law could have an impact on their program. These kinds of difficulties may need to be encountered and resolved many times before the law can be changed to accommodate your needs.

And the opposite is true. While they are being created, laws may get changed so much—accumulating exemptions and even unrelated amendments—that by the time they are passed they are virtually unrecognizable. They may not even do what you and your allies originally set out to accomplish. Moreover, laws are usually passed without money attached! Laws *authorize* spending state funds in many cases, but do not at the same time release (appropriate) the funds authorized; that comes later. At the time of appropriation, legislators may decide to fund the law in which you have an interest at far less than the level authorized—or even not at all. Legislators who sit on, or chair, appropriation committees exercise the real power of the purse in state government. As you probably have guessed, noncontroversial laws that have no fiscal implications are pretty easy to propose, get through the hearing process, and see into law.

State legislators are ordinary people. Many states, in fact, have what are called "citizen legislatures." That means that the members have regular jobs. Many, of course, will be lawyers, but many will not and most legislatures do include some educators. This is different from the federal legislature. In the U. S. Congress, members are "professional" lawmakers. At the federal level, serving in Congress is a fulltime job. In many states with citizen legislatures, the legislature is in session for only a few months each year. And in other states, the legislature doesn't even meet every year.

You and your coalition members can serve as important sources of information to legislators. Most legislators are very sensitive to the views of their constituents—and in this they are very much unlike officials at the state department of education, whose mandate takes in the whole state. Legislators actually represent particular communities at the state level.

When you give them feedback, especially feedback from a community group, you're playing a proper role; a role, in fact, intended at the founding of the country. The term *special interest group*, used unfavorably, though, refers to a different sort of feedback. Such special interest groups generally represent interests *outside* a geographic community. Their "special" interests have to do with professional or corporate objectives that are operating in many communities. Expression of these special interests is, of course, also proper—but often, the voices of these interests are heard not in proportion to their representation of the common good, but in proportion to how well financed they are. These sorts of special interest groups can be difficult even for large coalitions of average citizens to oppose effectively.

Legislators have to vote on so many different issues that they often vote blind, following someone else's lead, whether it is their party leader, an influential special interest group, or a colleague whose opinion they respect. So you can see that it is important for local communities to keep their legislatures informed. A citizen coalition with an interest in the local schools, one with staying power and a history of responsible concern, would not only exercise its democratic rights in maintaining close relations with its legislators—but would also serve as an example for other communities to follow.

**Governors.** Governors used to be fairly remote from educational issues, but this has changed dramatically within the past decade. The governors, for instance, collaborated in the framing and adoption of the National Education Goals, and they have been influential in creating goals for their own states, defining policy priorities, and proposing budgets to back up their agendas. Governors have considerable status and visibility that they can use to set the tone for discussions about education within a state. They also have significant bargaining power in the legislative process. They appoint people to leadership positions of every description, create special task forces and committees to recommend policy, and influence spending.

Governors, like other state-level players, work on a scale that tends to obscure local perspectives. Furthermore, they are besieged with problems, many of them having to do with finance. Provide your governor, if you can, with factual information and suggest effective solutions to problems that confront the state as a whole, and your interests may receive a serious hearing. And don't forget that governors, like other elected officials, tend to respond to voting blocs. If a large group of constituents endorses your interests, those interests are more likely to be considered important at the state level.

**State education agencies.** State departments of education are commonly referred to as SEAs (for *state education agency*). Most SEAs are large bureaucracies that arose from one-person offices established as a result of early reform efforts—beginning in the 1830s—by advocates like Horace Mann of Massachusetts. The federal constitution said (and says) nothing about education, and the early reformers were keen to establish the duty of a statewide entity to oversee a *system* of schools.

Subsequent legislation and constitutional activity in the states has tended to give state governments wide authority in creating, administering, and reforming the various state systems of education. This authority is exercised, in large measure, by the SEAs. Moreover, SEAs, partly under the guidance of the nation's governors, have increased their influence over how schools are run in recent decades.

The professionals who work at the SEA are not elected. They have jobs to do and they answer to their bosses, not to you. They play a difficult role. While they may be legally bound to provide you with certain kinds of information, they may not be aware that they are so bound. And even if they are, your inquiry may strike them as an interruption (it most likely *is* an interruption). But most people—even in large bureaucracies—want to serve the public as best they can. Give them a chance (see Box 5.3).

**Parents and citizens.** According to Carl Marburger, writing in 1985, "From total parent control of public education, we have come to almost no parent involvement; from one-room schools we have grown to multi-school districts and sprawling educational campuses" (p. 17).[1] Marburger's observations are as true today as when they were first written. Many parents believe that educators neither seek nor respect the counsel of parents. This sentiment is probably familiar to lots of people outside the school system. People involved professionally in education, by comparison to parents and citizens, have an organized place in the school system. They have a well-defined job to do and a structure for doing it.

---

[1] Marburger, C. L. (1985). *One school at a time*. Columbia, MD: National Committee for Citizens in Education. (ERIC Document Reproduction Service No. ED 263 683)

---

**Box 5.3**
**Cultivating the State Department of Education as a**
**Source of Information**

The state department of education (a.k.a. *state education agency* or *SEA*) controls much of the information about your school system statewide. The trick is how to get hold of the information you need. Your SEA is full of people who know only one area and, often, if you don't ask the right question, you won't get the information you need. We offer some basic tips from personal experience:

- SEA employees often wear many hats and carry out many tasks simultaneously. Think of them as potential sources of helpful information, rather than—if you are at all tempted in this direction—the enemy. Cultivate good relationships with those who are helpful.

- Find out who is in charge of public relations or public information for the SEA. If in doubt over whom to contact about which issues, ask this person.

- Get or compile a list of all the SEA positions that sound as if they are related to your interests.

- Don't be bashful: Keep calling. Mind your manners and keep your temper.

---

School reform plans increasingly stress the importance of involving parents and citizens or of ensuring their participation. This makes sense, because the same reforms that provide for more decision-making power for teachers often make room for parents and citizens. More and more, parents are being included in school improvement teams—and that, in fact, is the inspiration for this handbook.

But let's look at this thing the other way around. One could legitimately see this process of involvement or participation as one of helping *schools* improve the upbringing of children. It's a little crazy, isn't it, to talk about getting parents to participate in their children's education? After all, the parents—not the schools—do the child-rearing; parents are the parties fundamentally responsible here, not schools. Schools absolutely make a contribution to the upbringing of children, and the point of parent and citizen involvement is to increase the value of that contribution.

This puts a very different light on the situation. Schools can do a lot to bring parents into the loop—but parents and citizens must claim their own place in the life of the school as well. This is a difficult mission. They must contend with teachers and administrators who can claim information that is not available to citizens. They must overcome the implication that they are dealing in a professional field where they do not actually belong. And, along these lines, teachers have some reason to see parental involvement as a threat to their professional status. Such a reaction, of course, can be magnified by parents' possible insecurity about the value of their own contributions. That's why it can help if parents take the view that *they* are in charge of their own children's upbringing and that schooling needs to make the best possible addition to *their* efforts as parents. In taking this view, however, parents should avoid being arrogant or complacent. They can learn much from teachers and administrators, but not unless they actively cultivate mutually helpful relationships.

And the truth about "parental involvement" is that both perspectives apply—the usual one of school people that they need parents' help and the unusual one we've just described, that parents deserve the help of schools. What kids get out of school is improved if parents participate and if schools try better to respond to parents' efforts to do a good job.

Parents affect schools both individually and in groups. Individually, parents love their children, give children a basis for making significant commitments in their lives, provide secure environments to the extent of their ability, prepare their children for school, meet with teachers about their children's progress, vote in school board elections, and on and on. Nothing, in fact, can take the place of what parents can do in this way. Parents teach things that can hardly ever be taught or learned in school. For better or worse, parents are usually their children's most memorable and most effective teachers.

In groups, parents unite through service and interest groups (PTOs, band boosters, and so forth); they organize from time to time around particular issues (like textbook selection or school consolidation); and they join official advisory bodies (like parent advisory councils). One of the aims of this handbook is to increase the effectiveness of these sorts of groups. It is intended as a tool for group action across a variety of rural settings that will include both professionals and ordinary citizens.

CHAPTER 6

# Resources

T his handbook *is not* a cookbook. A cookbook gives you a recipe: Follow the recipe exactly and you'll get exactly what you expect. Getting involved with your small school, however, is nothing like baking a cake according to a recipe. When you get involved with schooling with your neighbors, you are taking action. Taking action can be nerveracking because no one on earth can assure you of the outcome.

And that's why we've included this chapter. It's here to show you that there is much more help available. Do not consider it a list of mandatory readings necessary for success. This chapter will lead you to printed materials, research tools, organizations, ideas—and people—that we could not possibly consider in enough detail between the covers of one book. Even here, we've had to make a very narrow selection of materials that we figured would be useful to a wide range of people. Still, it is a long list. Pick the items most useful to you and act!

## Topics Included

These are the major topics in this chapter:

- partnerships of parents, families, and communities with schools;

- building coalitions;

- needs assessment;

- the research literature about consolidation and school size;

- options featured in chapters 3 and 4 (Foxfire, rural enterprise, 4-day week, mixed-age grouping, and technology);

- *Pulling Together* (a compendium of rural education resources); and

- tools for finding information.

The last two sections take you beyond the particular ideas developed in this handbook.

The brief section called *Pulling Together* highlights a new resource portfolio compiled by the rural education programs of the 10 U. S. Department of Education's regional educational laboratories. It describes over 250 resources (a few are highlighted in this handbook) developed especially with the problems of small rural schools in view. This makes *Pulling Together* different from many resources listed in this chapter, which are necessarily "generic." In the first section, for instance, the works on parent, family, and community involvement are written for a national audience. They are all excellent—but none of them particularly address the unique circumstances of small and rural communities.

The final section aims to give you the tools to search for information independently—to become your own researcher, investigator, and originator of ideas.

## Partnerships of Parents, Families, and Communities With Schools

When families take an interest in children's schooling, the benefits are substantial. It's a fact, and research over three decades confirms it. Indeed, the power of parental involvement can be seen even at the national level—a dramatic example, for instance, can be seen in the revision of the National Education Goals. An eighth goal—increased parental involvement in learning—was added to the original list of six goals through the influence of the national Parent Teacher Association.

Community involvement strengthens the benefits that come from parental involvement. Most of the resources included here are concerned primarily with how to bring about effective partnerships. Most listings are 1990 or newer; a few from the 1980s are included because they are especially useful. Where bibliographies in publications are noteworthy, they are mentioned.

Barton, P., & Coley, R. (1992). *America's smallest school: The family (Policy Information Report).* Princeton, NJ: Educational Testing Service. (ERIC Document Reproduction Service No. ED 349 320)

Pulls together measures that reflect what goes on outside school and within the home in terms of educational achievement. Planners can use these numbers as indicators of what demands attention.

Burns, R. (Ed.). (1993). *Parents and schools: From visitors to partners.* West Haven, CT: National Education Association School Restructuring Series.

Provides models for creating effective school-home partnerships with full descriptions of three exemplary programs: *Family Connections,* an early childhood school-home communication tool; a process for parents as co-decision-makers and advocates at the secondary level; and a system to broaden parental roles in elementary school. A resource guide includes more than 100 listings of printed materials, workshops, and helpful organizations. Available from the NEA Professional Library, P.O. Box 509, West Haven, CT 06516. Credit card orders by phone 800/229-4200. For a free sample of *Family Connections,* call AEL at 800/624-9120.

Henderson, A., Marburger, C., & Ooms, T. (1986). *Beyond the bake sale: An educator's guide to working with parents.* Washington, DC: National Committee for Citizens in Education. (ERIC Document Reproduction Service No. ED 270 508)

Anne Henderson is one of the giants in parent involvement. Her annotated bibliography, *The Evidence Continues to Grow,* was published just a year after this guide, and the two books are key resources for individuals and groups who want home-school partnerships to be integral to their schools. The book is equally useful to parents, board of education members, and community members. A series of checklists helps you assess your school's characteristics, key characteristics of families in your school, and family-school relationships. The book went into a fifth printing in 1991. The National Committee for Citizens in Education (NCCE) is no longer in existence; however, their publications are available from The Center for Law and Education, 1875 Connecticut Avenue, NW, Suite 510, Washington, DC 20009; 202/462-7688.

Krupp, J., & Pauker, R. (1984). *When parents face the schools.* Manchester, CT: Adult Development and Learning.

This how-to book responds to several major questions parents most frequently have about schools: Who knows what about your child? Whom should you go to see in the school? What does your child learn in school? What are tests and what do they mean? Advises parents on understanding children's grades, helping them with homework, and other areas of concern. Includes a dictionary of education jargon, somewhat out of date but still useful. Ordering information is available from Adult Development and Learning, 40 McDivitt Drive, Manchester, CT 06040.

Melaville, A., & Blank, M. (1993). *Together we can*. Washington, DC: U. S. Department of Education and Department of Health and Human Services. (ERIC Document Reproduction Service No. ED 357 856)

*Together We Can: A Guide for Crafting a Profamily System of Education and Human Services* can assist local communities in the difficult process of creating a more responsive education and human service delivery system. Emphasis on families and community in planning for the best kind of educational experience. Includes a checklist-style process of crafting a profamily system of education and human services as well as an extensive directory of key contacts and organizational resources. The book is available from the U. S. Government Printing Office, Superintendent of Documents, Mail Stop SSOP, Washington, DC 20402-9328.

Meyers, E. (Ed.) (1989). *Teacher/parent partnerships handbook*. New York: Impact II.

This handbook is written for teachers by teachers, but parents will find it informative and insightful. It covers everything planners could need: setting goals for parent involvement, communicating with parents, organizing and scheduling techniques, integrating the school into the community, resources for teachers and parents, and developing partnerships with parents who have special needs. The single-copy price is $9.50; order from Impact II-The Teachers Network, P.O. Box 577, Canal Street Station, New York, NY 10012-0577; 212/966-5582.

Rich, D. (1985). *The forgotten factor in school success—the family* (A Policymaker's Guide). Washington, DC: The Home and School Institute.

Rich has been writing and producing materials on the importance of home and school working together for more than two decades. She says this publication provides "rationale, research, and supporting details for use in school-family programs and legislative initiatives, and in testimony, speeches, and campaign approaches." Much of her work has been done in partnership with the National Education Association, which has distributed her publications widely.

Other useful titles available from the Institute's MegaSkills Center, 1201 16th St. NW, Washington, DC 20036; 202/466-3633: *Families Learning Together, Survival Guide for Busy Parents, Bright Ideas,* and *Special Solutions.*

Smith, C. A., Cudaback, D., Goddard, H. W., & Myers-Walls, J. (1994). *National extension parent education model.* Manhattan, KS: Kansas Cooperative Extension Service.

Described by its authors as "a dynamic approach to parent education constructed through consensus." Includes an introduction and rationale, an in-depth description of the model, implementation steps, and a curriculum guide for infancy through early childhood. Visually pleasing and readable. Presents a blueprint for action that professionals and volunteers can use with ease. Includes descriptions of products from Extension Offices throughout the country. Extension Service increasingly offers education and other help through a model that supports integrated services delivery. Contact your local agent for more information.

United States Department of Education. (1994). *Strong families, strong schools.* Washington, DC: Author. (ERIC Document Reproduction Service No. ED 371 909)

A research base for family involvement in education that provides how-to on building community partnerships. Includes an extensive reference section. Available free in single copies by calling 800/USA-LEARN (800/872-5327). Your name will then be on a mailing list for a monthly newsletter from the U. S. Department of Education: *Goals 2000 Community Update.*

Walker, S. F., & Lindner, B. (1988). *Drawing in the family.* Denver, CO: Education Commission of the States. (ERIC Document Reproduction Service No. ED 298 197)

One of the most practical, easy-to-use publications in a rapidly growing stack about parent involvement. Sets forth expectations, barriers, and opportunities for connecting families and schools, and provides suggestions for improving both home and school environments. Describes some successful programs and concludes with strategies for state action. Copies are available for $12.00 each from the ECS Distribution Center, 1860 Lincoln Street, Suite 300, Denver, CO 80295; 303/830-3692.

## Building Coalitions

The resources listed next give similar information about how to form effective coalitions. Some are written for administrators wishing to build community support for school issues or programs; others are written for people in the community wishing to support and improve their schools. All are brief, practical, relatively inexpensive, and available through ERIC (see the last part of this chapter, "Tools for Finding Information," for a description of how to get help from ERIC, the federally funded Educational Resources Information Center).

California Congress of Parents, Teachers, and Students and the California State Department of Education. (1981). *A guide to school and community action.* Sacramento, CA: California State Department of Education. (ERIC Document Reproduction Service No. ED 208 316)

> Information about coalition building is in an appendix of this action guide in workbook format. The guide describes a 4-step process of (1) conducting a needs assessment, (2) organizing the community, (3) developing an action plan, and (4) implementing and evaluating the plan.

Education Commission of the States. (1993). *What communities should know and be able to do about education.* Denver, CO: Author. (ERIC Document Reproduction Service No. ED 360 684)

> This workbook, like the previous citation, offers a step-by-step process for building support and taking action. One chapter provides examples of how states and communities have used the community-building process described in the workbook to restructure their education systems. Examples come from Alaska, Arkansas, Connecticut, Indiana, South Carolina, and Vermont.

Hart, T. (1988). *Building coalitions for support of schools.* Eugene, OR: Oregon School Study Council. (ERIC Document Reproduction Service No. ED 297 482)

> Directed to school superintendents, the bulletin discusses the value of coalitions and gives steps for forming them. It also includes examples of coalitions in action.

Jackson, D., & Maddy, W. (1992). *Building coalitions.* Columbus, OH: Ohio State University. (ERIC Document Reproduction Service No. ED 350 407)

This series of 16 fact sheets provides information on topics related to coalition development. Each ends with a summary and list of references.

Livermore, A., Roth, L., & Stamm, C. (1986). *How to form and operate a local alliance: A handbook for local action to improve science and technology education.* Washington, DC: National Science Teachers Association. (ERIC Document Reproduction Service No. ED 307 169)

Although this guide's title refers to science and technology education, the information applies to forming coalitions in general. Topics include alliance composition, needs, goals, priorities, funding, programs and projects, evaluation, communications, and publicity.

Maine Association for Supervision and Curriculum Development. (1992). *Beyond tinkering: Transformation; a community plan for helping all children learn.* Augusta, ME: Author. (ERIC Document Reproduction Service No. ED 353 072)

Narrow in focus, but useful for developing consensus, this is a facilitator's guide for a meeting in which people with differing views can establish a common vision and good working relationships.

Martin-McCormick, L., Millsap, M., Blum, C., Burton, C., & Lecar, H. (1982). *Organizing for change: PEER's guide to campaigning for equal education.* (1982). Washington, DC: National Organization for Women. (ERIC Document Reproduction Service No. ED 240 183)

Intended for an audience of parents and local community members, this manual is in a workbook format. In addition to information about forming and managing coalitions, guidance is provided for working effectively in groups and for fundraising. Like the previous citation, the information applies to forming coalitions in general, even though the title specifies a particular focus.

Thomas, J., Hart, T., & Smith, S. (1989). *Building coalitions.* Eugene, OR: ERIC Clearinghouse on Educational Management. (ERIC Document Reproduction Service No. ED 309 516)

This document is chapter 12 in *School Leadership: Handbook for Excellence.* It discusses ways for administrators to enlist community support through coalition building. Chapter sections are on initiating and operating a coalition and obtaining the support of key groups.

Webb, K., Ludlow, B., & Ristow, B. (1992). *A guide to resources on advocacy: Facts, strategies and information.* Indianapolis, IN: Indiana Youth Institute. (ERIC Document Reproduction Service No. ED 367 445)

This guide aims to improve the effectiveness of child advocates. Although aimed at Indiana residents, it includes ideas related to coalition-building in general. A section on strategies, for instance, lists 60 ways to be an advocate. The guide also contains a useful bibliography of books on youth advocacy.

## Needs Assessment

As indicated in chapter 5 (see Box 5.1), "needs" describe desires or aspirations. In any complex project, developing an overview of these matters is critical. A good overview will *describe* systematically the existing needs as participants see them. A completed needs assessment, moreover, helps a group *prioritize* and *justify* its needs. Prioritized needs give other people, as well as your own group, a more-or-less balanced perspective for deciding what the project needs to do.

Engaging in a process to assess needs helps bring together the different perceptions that individuals have. The needs assessment process itself, therefore, turns private (subjective) perceptions into public (or objective) "needs." That's why assessing needs in a systematic way is so important. It lets people know that you "have your act together"—and it tells them just what that act is.

There are many ways to conduct a systematic assessment of needs. You can conduct a survey, hold meetings, and apply a variety of other tools to gather and analyze what you discover (the data). Data analysis will usually require some statistical expertise, and a consultant (or a volunteer with consulting experience) will be needed. This person should be involved in planning and designing the needs assessment process from the very beginning.

Needs assessment is part of the planning that organizations do for many different purposes, as well. Your purpose—whether you are making long-term or short-term plans, designing a program or a proposal, or just trying to build consensus—will make a difference in how you design and carry out a needs assessment.

The resources that follow should give you an idea of the range of possibilities and some sense of the variety of tools you can use. Some of these resources consider the idea or use of needs assessment, generally, whereas others discuss particular methods and tools for actually conducting formal needs assessments. Still others offer good examples of the results of using a needs assessment process. Most of the resources are available directly from the ERIC Document Reproduction Service or in journal articles (see the final section of this chapter). For other items, ordering information is provided.

Coleman, D., & Lawrence, J. (1984). Switching school board function to a futuristic orientation. *Rural Educator, 6*(1), 1-2.

To help school boards respond to the rising median population age and emerging high-tech society, this article suggests school boards separate from day-to-day administrative operations and concentrate on futuristic five-year plans. Would help provide optimal accountability and improved preparedness.

Everett, R., & Sloan, C. (1984). School board orientation: Rural vs urban. *Small School Forum, 5*(2), 7-9.

Reports the results of a survey to collect information on training and orientation programs for school board members. Results indicated a need for increased orientation and training programs.

Flora, C., & Christenson, J. (Eds.). (1991). *Rural policies for the 1990s* (Rural Studies Series). Boulder, CO: Westview Press.

This book contains 27 chapters by a variety of authors considered to be experts on rural America. The book focuses on policy-relevant research on the problems of rural areas. In each chapter, rural policy needs are identified by examining the flow of events and rural sociology of the 1980s. (Available from the publisher, 5500 Central Avenue, Boulder, CO 80301-2847, paperback $24.95.)

Hansen, B., & Marburger, C. (1988). *School based improvement: A manual for district leaders.* Columbia, MD: National Committee for Citizens in Education. (ERIC Document Reproduction Service No. ED 301 954)

This manual reviews (as of 1988) the literature on school-based improvement processes. But it also interprets the roles of the various actors to be involved—including parents and community. An appendix includes examples of needs assessment instruments.

Hoke, G. (1983). The pitfalls of needs assessments. *Research in Rural Education, 2*(1), 39-41.

Discusses problems encountered by rural officials in conducting needs assessments of community services and their implications for policymakers.

Langone, C. (1990, February). *Critical issue identification: A vital step for rural leadership.* Paper presented at the annual meeting of the Southern Rural Sociological Society, Little Rock, AR. (ERIC Document Reproduction Service No. ED 325 277)

This paper describes the use of the nominal group technique as a tool to assist community leaders in 23 Georgia counties, most of them rural, in identifying and prioritizing community issues.

Mann, G., Price, J., & Kellogg, D. (1993, November). *Rural secondary school science teachers: What they need to be successful.* Paper presented at the annual meeting of the Mid-South Educational Research Association, New Orleans, LA. (ERIC Document Reproduction Service No. ED 366 472)

This document reports the results of a survey of 1,507 science teachers in six different states. It is an example of how to use a survey to develop a picture of needs. The data show that science teachers in rural schools have many needs that differ from those in more urbanized areas and reveal what is needed to improve instruction and student performance in science education.

National Education Association. (1944). *The White House Conference on Rural Education (October 3-5).* Washington, DC: Author. (ERIC Document Reproduction Service No. ED 347 004)

This booklet provides a historical benchmark for considering rural education needs. It presents the proceedings of a 1944 conference on rural education, held in the White House with Eleanor Roosevelt participating. The conference prepared a Charter of Education for Rural Children containing 10 educational rights of the rural child. The conference provided a variety of speakers addressing a variety of problems facing rural education.

Reed, D. F., & Seyfarth, J. T. (1984). Assessing teacher needs in rural schools. *Rural Educator, 6*(1), 12-17.

Focuses on a study that took place in a remote, rural, mid-Atlantic school system that assessed how teachers regarded the curriculum and their instructional needs. Data were gathered through interviews, a questionnaire, and classroom observations.

Roblyer, M. (Ed.). (1986). *A model for assessing and meeting needs in instructional computing: Procedures and results of a multi-state needs assessment.* Tallahassee, FL: Florida Association of Educational Data Systems. (ERIC Document Reproduction Service No. ED 274 321)

This report describes a needs assessment process used widely by the Appalachia Educational Laboratory (AEL) and others. The process is known as the DAP—for "descriptive-appraisive-prescriptive." This report is about a particular application of the process, but it describes the process used, and an appendix includes the participants' manual. See reports that bear the ERIC Document Reproduction Service Numbers ED 315 211 and ED 299 292 for other examples of how the DAP has been used.

Schmidt, G. L. (1983). Developing effective staff development programs in rural school systems. *Small School Forum, 5*(1), 15-16.

Notes the traditional budget problems with rural school staff development. Focuses on how the In-Service Council, a quality circle method used by rural schools in Dansville, New York, advises the administration on staff development programs, based on needs assessments.

Shroyer, G., & Enochs, L. (1986). Strategies for assessing the unique strengths, needs, and visions of rural science teachers. *Research in Rural Education, 4*(1), 39-43.

This article discusses strategies for assessing needs related to the development of a proposal to the National Science Foundation for funding to improve rural science education.

Vaughan, M., & Morris, P. (1990, March). *The rural Southwest in the year 2002: Implications for educational policy.* Paper presented at the Rural Education Symposium of the American Council on Rural Special Education and the National Rural and Small Schools Consortium, Tucson, AZ. (ERIC Document Reproduction Service No. ED 337 325)

This report describes issues forums that examined the conditions and needs of rural and small schools in five states. Participants were assigned by role to groups and used the nominal group technique to identify priorities for rural education and develop an action plan to address each top priority.

# The Research Literature About Consolidation and School Size

The research literature on consolidation and school size is very large, with over 400 articles, reports, and other types of documents indexed in ERIC (see "Tools for Finding Information," which appears last in this chapter). For the most part, ERIC resources go back only to the year 1966, and, of course, studies were conducted back as far as the early years of the century. The resources selected here, however, are the ones that represent the current state of knowledge and that are most useful to people who need to understand the issues that are relevant now.

Missing from this list are the earlier resources (less relevant to action in the present) that give the bigger-is-better argument. It is interesting to see what the arguments were and, in fact, to see how different the world of, say, 1920 or 1940 was from the world of 1997 or 2000. The world does not stand still, and that is one of the reasons why thinking about issues such as school size has to change (and is changing).

The research literature is not easy to read. We've summarized the findings of each listed resource very briefly. If you know something about statistics, however, and enjoy reading nonfiction, take a look at some of the full-length studies. The resources in this section of the chapter are separated by form: Books in one set and research articles (from professional journals) in a separate set.

ERIC Digests summarize portions of the professional literature for a wide audience; listed below, for instance, is a Digest on achievement and school size (Howley, 1994). See "Tools for Finding Information" at the end of this chapter for more details about ERIC Digests.

### Books

Barker, R., & Gump, P. (1964). *Big school, small school.* Palo Alto, CA: Stanford University Press.

This book is one of the classic studies comparing small and large schools. It was written for an academic audience. The key finding is that, since small schools do most of the things large schools do, each student is called upon more frequently to take part in school roles and functions. Students are more firmly attached to small than to large schools. (*Big School, Small School* is out of print, but you can borrow a copy from a library; if not available locally, ask for an "interlibrary loan.")

Brown, R. (1991). *Schools of thought: How the politics of literacy shape thinking in the classroom.* San Francisco: Jossey-Bass.

This book is not principally about small schools, but it talks a lot about what education should be—the themes of knowledge, skills, and understanding dealt with in chapter 2. It's very readable, and it does give examples of the way that large school and district size can get in the way of a good education. ($14.95, paperback, from Jossey-Bass, 350 Sansome Street, San Francisco, CA 94104; 415/433-1767)

Conant, J. (1959). *The American high school today: A first report to citizens.* New York: McGraw-Hill.

James Conant was a chemistry professor, and later president, of Harvard University. This book rallied Americans, in the era of Sputnik, to close small high schools across the country. It gives the traditional arguments for closure: talent development for national security, improved curriculum, and cost efficiency. Conant believed that a high school had to graduate *at least* 100 students a year to be effective; that is, 9-12 high schools should enroll at least 400 students. Schools about twice this size were optimal. (As with the Barker and Gump volume, you'll have to borrow this from a library; but so many copies of this book were circulated that it will be much easier to locate than *Big School, Small School.*)

DeYoung, A. (1995). *The life and death of a rural American high school: Farewell, Little Kanawha.* New York: Garland.

This book is a close-up look at a rural community and the fate of one of its high schools over many decades. A particular concern is the relationship between what the rural community thinks and the professional view that increasingly influences what happens at the school. Consolidation is a major theme. ($50.00, hard cover only, 717 Fifth Avenue, Suite 2500, New York, NY 10022; 800/627-6273)

Nachtigal, P. (Ed.). (1982). *Rural education: In search of a better way.* Boulder, CO: Westview Press.

This book takes the view that schools and communities in rural areas are closely tied and argues that a high level of local involvement is essential when improvement plans are made. The 13 case studies included demonstrate the point. The final chapters analyze the case studies in practical terms and recommend policy and practice for future rural school improvement. (Also out of print; consult a library.)

Schmuck, R., & Schmuck, P. (1992). *Small districts, big problems: Making school everybody's house.* Newbury Park, CA: Corwin Press.

This book tells the story of the authors' visits to 80 rural, small schools in 21 states. They found that each school—almost all in places experiencing deep economic hardship—was a community center. But the authors were surprised to find bored students, regimentation, authoritarianism, and overworked and frustrated teachers. The final chapter presents ideas about how to change these conditions. ($18.95, paperback, from Corwin Press, Inc., 2455 Teller Rd., Newbury Park, CA 91320; 805/499-0721)

Sher, J. (Ed.). (1981). *Rural education in urbanized nations: Issues and innovations (OECD/CERI Report).* Boulder, CO: Westview Press.

This volume is designed to provide a foundation of information and insights on education in the sparsely populated areas of a group of industrialized nations. Small school size is among the key topics considered; the book also addresses rural education issues generally. Countries considered include Portugal, New Zealand, Scotland, Australia, Finland, Norway, and the United States. (Out of print, but available through libraries.)

### Research Articles and Summaries

DeYoung, A., Howley, C., & Theobald, P. (1995). The cultural contradictions of middle schooling for rural community survival. *Journal of Research in Rural Education, 11*(1), 24-35.

This article finds that the overall effect of the "middle school movement" has contributed nationwide to school closures in rural areas. This trend has not only helped create large elementary and high schools, but has also sorted students into increasingly narrow age ranges. The K-8 elementary school is becoming a thing of the past in rural areas. Consolidations also threaten the continuing existence of rural communities.

Fetler, M. (1989). School dropout rates, academic performance, size, and poverty: Correlates of educational reform. *Educational Evaluation and Policy Analysis, 11*(2), 109-116.

This article finds that large schools serve poor students badly. It also shows that high dropout rates (a real problem in large urban schools serving impoverished students) coincide with low achievement *among the students who remain in school.* Large schools can foster a climate of underachievement.

117

Fowler, W. (1992, April). *What do we know about school size? What should we know?* Paper presented at the annual meeting of the American Educational Research Association, San Francisco. (ERIC Document Reproduction Service No. ED 347 675)

This is perhaps *the best available overall review* of the literature on school size, even though it has never been published in a journal. The author concludes that large size is bad for student attitudes, participation, and attendance; and that, once socioeconomic status is considered, small schools and districts produce higher achievement.

Fowler, W., & Walberg, H. (1991). School size, characteristics, and outcomes. *Educational Evaluation and Policy Analysis, 13*(2), 189-202.

This study looked at information about high schools in New Jersey. It found that, with socioeconomic status controlled, smaller schools and districts do a better job of helping high school students learn.

Friedkin, N., & Necochea, J. (1988). School system size and performance: A contingency perspective. *Educational Evaluation and Policy Analysis, 10*(3), 237-249.

This study found that socioeconomic status (SES) regulates the effects of school and district size on students' achievement (at least with the data from California used by the researchers). Low-SES students do much better in small than in large schools, they found. However, high-SES students do somewhat better in large than in small schools.

Haller, E. (1992). High school size and student indiscipline: Another aspect of the school consolidation issue? *Educational Evaluation and Policy Analysis, 14*(2), 145-156.

This article looks at student "indiscipline"—truancy and disorder (e.g., assaults against teachers)—and finds that large schools, even in rural areas, have higher levels of indiscipline. It suggests, however, that, in rural areas nationwide, doubling the average size of high schools (from 443 to 886) will not increase indiscipline very much. In some areas, of course, rural high schools are a good deal larger than this already. Haller suggests that community preferences should determine whether consolidation occurs, because neither equity, efficiency, nor discipline offer a good reason to close small schools.

Haller, E., Monk, D., Spotted Bear, A., Griffith, J., & Moss, P. (1990). School size and program comprehensiveness: Evidence from high school and beyond. *Educational Evaluation and Policy Analysis, 12*(2), 109-120.

This study shows that offering a "broad curriculum" cannot be assured by making schools bigger. For one thing, schools seem to add new courses unevenly across the curriculum—the rate at which new courses are added vary by subject area. The curriculum doesn't get expanded across the board all at once. Very small high schools cannot offer a comprehensive curriculum but, on average, schools with only 400 students offer a substantial and comprehensive program.

Haller, E., Monk, D., & Tien, L. (1993). Small schools and higher-order thinking skills. *Journal of Research in Rural Education, 9*(2), 66-73.

This study considered the possibility that small schools might not do very well in cultivating the kinds of "high-level" thinking that many standardized, norm-referenced achievement tests (traditional tests) don't measure. The researchers, however, found that there is no difference between small and large schools.

Howley, C. (1989). Synthesis of the effects of school and district size: What research says about achievement in small schools and school districts. *Journal of Rural and Small Schools, 4*(1), 2-12.

This review concludes that small schools and districts generally provide achievement advantages, especially for impoverished children. It also notes that early studies based on findings about achievement recommended that schools be about half as large as studies based on such things as course offerings.

Howley, C. (1994). *The academic effectiveness of small-scale schooling (an update)* (ERIC Digest EDO-RC-94-1). Charleston, WV: ERIC Clearinghouse on Rural Education and Small Schools. (ERIC Document Reproduction Service No. ED 372 897)

This two-page summary of recent research discusses most of the studies described in this list of resources. It considers the development of the literature, the issue of attainment (how far people go in school), issues related to high schools, and the idea of community.

Huang, G., & Howley, C. (1993). Mitigating disadvantage: Effects of small-scale schooling on students' achievement in Alaska. *Journal of Research in Rural Education, 9*(3), 137-149.

This study provides more evidence that small school size benefits disadvantaged students. It found that small size reduces the negative effects of coming from a disadvantaged background, but large size increases them. The study also found some evidence that the influence of size depends on community socioeconomic status.

Kleinfeld, J., McDiarmid, G., & Hagstrom, D. (1989). Small local high schools decrease Alaska Native drop-out rates. *Journal of American Indian Education, 28*(3), 24-30.

The authors present data to show that Alaska's very small village high schools serve Alaska Native students much better than the large boarding schools that previously enrolled many village youth.

Monk, D., Haller, E., & Bail, J. (1986). *Secondary school enrollment and curricular comprehensiveness.* Ithaca, NY: Cornell University. (ERIC Document Reproduction Service No. ED 287 628)

This study concluded that schools often do not make good on the opportunities for improving the curriculum that large size is supposed to offer. Large schools *can* theoretically offer a broad curriculum, but often they fail to do so. The authors observe that a high school that enrolls about 400 students (total) is really large enough to offer a sufficiently broad curriculum.

Nimnicht, G., & Partridge, A. (1962). *Small schools can be good schools.* Greeley, CO: Colorado State College, Educational Planning Service. (ERIC Document Reproduction Service No. ED 231 553)

This report, now more than 30 years old, is included here to demonstrate that interest in the benefits of small-scale schooling is longstanding. The authors surveyed 37 small high schools in 22 states, with enrollments ranging from 27 to 328. The report includes a discussion of how the schools worked to offer the "diverse curriculum" that educational experts seem to value. Note that the schools studied have enrollments less than the 400 recommended by James Conant as a minimum—and cited by Monk and colleagues as the level at which a "comprehensive" curriculum can be rather easily achieved.

Pittman, R., & Haughwout, P. (1987). Influence of high school size on dropout rate. *Educational Evaluation and Policy Analysis, 9*(4), 337-43.

This study looked at dropout rate, school climate, program diversity, and size. The researchers found that larger schools have higher dropout rates, principally because of poorer school climate. More-over, they found that a broad and diverse curriculum reduces the dropout rate by only a small amount.

Plecki, M. (1991, April). *The relationship between elementary school size and student achievement.* Paper presented at the annual meeting of the American Educational Research Association, Chicago, IL.

This study looked at achievement, school size, and location (rural, suburban, urban) among elementary schools in California. It found that larger size is not associated with better student performance, and that the negative size-achievement relationship was more of a prob-lem in urban than in rural schools.

Sergiovanni, T. (1993, April). *Organizations or communities? Changing the metaphor changes the theory.* Paper presented at the annual meeting of the American Educational Research Association, Atlanta, GA. (ERIC Document Reproduction Service No. ED 376 008)

This paper is a "think piece" about the ideas of community and organization. A school should be a community, not an organization, says the author. And, he says, community can exist only in small schools; no school, he insists, should enroll more than 300 students. This author's work is cited many times in the field of educational administration.

Toenjes, L. (1989). *Dropout rates in Texas school districts: Influences of school size and ethnic group.* Austin, TX: Texas Center for Educational Research. (ERIC Document Reproduction Service No. ED 324 783)

This study finds that high dropout rates (in Texas) are not primarily a problem among nonwhites, and that large school size is a serious threat to continuing in school for all ethnic groups. The problem may be the worst, according to this study, among white students in large urban districts.

Walberg, H. (1989). District size and student learning. *Education and Urban Society, 21*(2), 154-163.

This study found that, when the influence of both socioeconomic status and expenditure per student were taken into account, there was a negative relationship between district size and average student achievement in the district. Students had lower achievement in larger districts.

Walberg, H., & Fowler, W. (1987). Expenditure and size efficiencies of public school districts. *Educational Researcher, 16*(7), 5-13.

The point of this study was to find out which districts (in New Jersey) could increase achievement beyond what would be expected from their families' socioeconomic origins (SES). Without controlling for SES, affluent districts, as expected, did better than impoverished districts. And larger districts spent more per pupil than smaller districts. But with socioeconomic status controlled, students in the smaller districts (New Jersey has over 600 separate districts) were shown to achieve better than students in large districts (at lower per-pupil cost).

Wihry, D., Coladarci, T., & Meadow, C. (1992). Grade span and eighth-grade academic achievement: Evidence from a predominantly rural state. *Journal of Research in Rural Education, 8*(2), 58-70.

This unique study looked at the grades that make up schools and asked if that had anything to do with achievement, specifically the achievement of eighth graders. This is a good question, since K-8 schools are going out of style, in favor of K-4, K-6, and middle schools. The findings suggest that eighth-grade students do best in K-8 schools, worse in middle-level schools, and worst of all in 7-12 schools.

## Options Featured in Chapters 3 and 4

This section includes additional resources about the specific options featured in chapters 3 and 4: (1) Foxfire and similar efforts, (2) rural enterprise, (3) the 4-day week, (4) mixed-age grouping, and (5) technology. Please keep in mind, again, that none of these options is in any way a "magic bullet."

In fact, the point of this section is to help you consider these options in greater depth—looking for things that may be most relevant for your school and your community. Remember that part of the reason we featured these options is that there is a substantial literature on each: Many people have tried these alternatives and written about their experiences. This fact still doesn't guarantee that any of them will work in your situation. The most important part of each, and it's sometimes easy to forget this, is the people behind the projects.

**Foxfire, Experiential Education, and Related Efforts**

Appalshop. (1992). *Appalshop film and video on culture and social issues.* Whitesburg, KY: Author. (ERIC Document Reproduction Service No. ED 357 932)

This collection of 76 award-winning films and videos focuses on people from southern Appalachia and their lifestyles. Seven of the education entries portray rural and one-room schools, school reform efforts, and the Foxfire approach in a second grade classroom. (Contact Appalshop at 306 Madison Street, Whitesburg, KY 41858; 606/633-0108 or 800/545-7467.)

Casto, J. (1991). Networking works for eastern Kentucky schools. *Appalachia, 24*(1), 22-25.

This article describes the Eastern Kentucky Teachers' Network (EKTN), developed by the Foxfire Teacher Outreach program for training teachers in the Foxfire approach to education.

Easton, S. (1985, October). *Social studies and citizenship education in rural America: Process and product.* Paper presented at the National Conference on Rural Teacher Education, Bellingham, WA. (ERIC Document Reproduction Service No. ED 261 847)

This paper reviews 33 studies about social studies education and indicates that the process and the outcome of social studies education in rural communities is not very different from that in the rest of the country. Despite the excitement surrounding the "Foxfire" program and the efforts of curriculum innovators, students in rural America are likely to encounter a rather ordinary social studies program.

Foxfire Foundation. *The Active Learner* (formerly *Hands On*). (50 issues published through March 1995)

*The Active Learner* is the magazine of the Foxfire Foundation's Teacher Outreach program. Each issue contains many articles by teachers, about teaching, for teachers—and for those interested in experiential learning generally. (Contact Foxfire Outreach, P. O. Box 541, Mountain City, GA 30562; 706/746-5828.) This unusual magazine is currently abstracted by the ERIC Clearinghouse on Rural Education and Small Schools; over 90 items related to this magazine are abstracted in the ERIC database.

Gingerich, O. (1992). Filling the experience gap in the information age. *Camping Magazine, 64*(5), 25-28.

This article focuses on the importance of children putting the theory they have learned through formal education into practice. It discusses how outdoor education offers learning experiences that integrate experience and information.

Olmstead, K. (1989). *Touching the past, en route to the future: Cultural journalism in the curriculum of rural schools* (ERIC Digest). Charleston, WV: ERIC Clearinghouse on Rural Education and Small Schools. (ERIC Document Reproduction Service No. ED 308 057)

This digest describes the development of cultural journalism and its place in the contemporary curriculum. The digest examines the forms cultural journalism can take such as courses, magazines, newspapers, or anthologies, as well as video, tapes, records, and radio and television productions.

Stoops, J. (1993). *The use of peer-based support in rural settings to effect curriculum renewal.* Portland, OR: Northwest Regional Educational Laboratory. (ERIC Document Reproduction Service No. ED 363 489)

This handbook discusses how five professional teacher networks expand available resources through the collective efforts of network members. Teachers in small, rural schools reported that these networks had significant positive impact on curriculum renewal. The networks also provided teachers with the professional benefits of collegial relationships, reduced professional isolation, supported individual classroom practices, and provided access to field tested materials and information.

Weible, T. (1984). Using community resources to enhance the rural school curriculum. *Small School Forum, 5*(2), 13-14.

This article describes a variety of community-related activities that can help establish greater relevance and meaning of community life for rural students.

## Rural Enterprise

Baker, K. (1990). *Rural school-based enterprise: Promise and practice in the Southeast*. Research Triangle Park: Southeast Educational Improvement Laboratory. (ERIC Document Reproduction Service No. ED 330 513)

> This document discusses the concept of the school-based enterprise (SBE) program. The appendices summarize SBE program objectives, list "dos" and "don'ts" for project success, and briefly describe 25 projects in North Carolina, South Carolina, and Georgia.

Gatewood, E., & DeLargy, P. (1985). *School-based businesses in Georgia*. Unpublished paper. (ERIC Document Reproduction Service No. ED 279 477; see also ED 303 302 and ED 277 853 for related works)

> This paper discusses a school-based business program in Georgia that is attempting to broaden the education of high school students by making them more aware of the role of small business in the United States economy and the economic possibilities offered by entrepreneurship. It also discusses program goals, the variety of school-based businesses started in Georgia, and the problems encountered.

Hobbs, D. (1987). *Learning to find the "niches": Rural education and vitalizing rural communities*. Elmhurst, IL: North Central Regional Educational Laboratory. (ERIC Document Reproduction Service No. ED 301 365)

> This document discusses how rural America has undergone substantial restructuring that affects rural education and prospects for rural economic development. The author suggests that new rural development strategies should consider the job-creating potential of small business and entrepreneurship, the importance of knowledge-based enterprise, and the need to create new networks and partnerships to support avenues of alternative development. He also suggests that rural schools must provide sound basic education and train students to be innovative, to have multiple skills, and to work as members of small problem-solving teams.

Paquin, T. (1991). A school-based enterprise: The Saint Pauls, North Carolina, experience. *Rural Special Education Quarterly, 10*(4), 26-28.

> The superintendent of Saint Pauls Schools describes how educators, community leaders, business people, and high school students worked together to develop a successful business.

Rosenfeld, S. (1983). Something old, something new: The wedding of rural education and rural development. *Phi Delta Kappan, 65*(4), 270-73. (Also available on ERIC microfiche as ERIC Document Reproduction Service No. ED 261 815)

This article describes how updated vocational agricultural programs and school-based enterprises can help rebuild rural economies. It explains the feasibility of this concept. (Part of a theme issue on rural education that appeared in this major education journal.)

Trujillo, F. (1988, September). *Rural schools and community development: A conceptual design project.* Paper presented at the annual meeting of the National Rural Education Association, Bismarck, ND. (ERIC Document Reproduction Service No. ED 332 833)

This document offers a synthesis and overview from experts in rural community, rural education, and economic development who were invited to participate in a mini-conference on rural schools and community development.

Wall, M., & Luther, V. (1988). *Schools as entrepreneurs: Helping small towns survive.* Lincoln, NE: Heartland Center for Leadership Development. (ERIC Document Reproduction Service No. ED 312 097)

This booklet reports findings of a national research project to identify innovative school-based business projects. Seven schools were chosen for the range of innovative and promising school-based businesses they represented. The booklet also examines legal considerations and enterprise selection and planning, and provides 10 strategies for school-based economic development. (Contact Heartland at 941 O Street, Suite 920, Lincoln, NE 68508; 402/474-7667 or 800/927-1115.)

## Four-day Week

Anderson, J. (1983). An alternative to the four-day week. *Small School Forum, 4*(3), 19-21.

This article describes how Gunnison Watershed School District shortened the school year by adding 26 minutes to each school day, thus eliminating 12 days from the standard 180 days required.

Bauman, P. (1983). *The four-day school week* (Issuegram 14). Denver, CO: Education Commission of the States. (ERIC Document Reproduction Service No. ED 234 502)

This document discusses the pros and cons of a 4-day school week. It lists six points to be considered when contemplating a change to the 4-day week—state legislation, implications for energy usage, calendar changes, providing for activities and special instruction, applying research knowledge about learning and instruction, and getting input from all concerned.

Brubacher, R., & Stiverson, C. (1982). *Colorado's alternative school calendar program and the four-day week.* Denver, CO: Colorado State Department of Education. (ERIC Document Reproduction Service No. ED 214 719)

This document reports the results of a study conducted by Colorado State University on the 13 original school districts using the 4-day school week. It also reports negative factors concluded from other observations and studies.

Culbertson, J. (1982). *Four-day school week for small rural schools* (Small Schools Fact Sheet). Las Cruces, NM: ERIC Clearinghouse on Rural Education and Small Schools. (ERIC Document Reproduction Service No. ED 232 799)

The author explains the concept of a 4-day school week, focusing on the positive aspects and reporting that only a few minor negative aspects have been reported from the 12 Colorado school districts and 20 colleges that have tried it.

Daly, J., & Richburg, R. (1984). *Student achievement in the four-day school week.* (ERIC Document Reproduction Service No. ED 252 346)

This report discusses the results and implications of a study conducted to gather longitudinal student achievement data from schools utilizing the 4-day week.

Koki, S. (1992). *Modified school schedules: A look at the research and the Pacific.* Honolulu, HI: Pacific Region Educational Laboratory. (ERIC Document Reproduction Service No. ED 354 630)

Some small, rural districts in Hawaii have begun to use the 4-day school week, with a longer school day. This report describes the advantages and opportunities such a change involves. Achievement gains are reported.

Like, C. D. (1994). Perspectives: Implementing the modified four-day school week. *The Alberta Journal of Educational Research, 40*(3), 271-281.

> This article describes the development and initial experience with moving a 500-student junior high school to a "modified" 4-day week (every other week is a 4-day week). It discusses motives, involvement of community, and surprises.

Monk, D. (1988). *Disparities in curricular offerings: Issues and policy alternatives for small, rural schools* (Policy Issues). (ERIC Document Reproduction Service No. ED 307 096)

> This review explores the debate on optimal school size and discusses policy options available to states for expanding curricular offerings in small, rural schools. The document pays particular attention to the possibilities associated with residential schools (the traditional approach), locally designed reorganizations (the modified traditional approach), and the use of instructional technologies (the nontraditional approach).

Sagness, R., & Salzman, S. (1993, October). *Evaluation of the four-day school week in Idaho suburban schools.* Paper presented at the annual meeting of the Northern Rocky Mountain Educational Research Association, Jackson, WY. (ERIC Document Reproduction Service No. ED 362 995)

> This study looked at absenteeism, student achievement, costs, and classroom activity. There was no decrease in student achievement, there were cost savings, absenteeism declined (for both students and staff), and students' engaged time in the classroom increased. After a year the district abandoned the 4-day week, according to the authors, because of administrative problems.

School fits three R's into four days. (1983, June 9). *Sun News*, p. 12a. (ERIC Document Reproduction Service No. ED 242 443)

> *The following is the full text of this document*: The last bell rings at 4 o'clock and kids come tumbling out of classrooms, eager to be free for the weekend. As lockers bang shut and chatter fades out the front door, one teacher sighs, "Thank God it's Thursday." Thursday? For the 250 students and 16 teachers in this southwestern Oregon farming community, Thursday marks the end of the school week in an experimental program that packs the three R's into four days. Started last

fall to save money on heating, lighting, and busing, the four-day school week appeals to teachers who enjoy long weekends and parents who say their children are more enthusiastic about school. "We're still on a trial basis," said Bob Brown, chairman of the Days Creek school board. "But we haven't had one complaint to the board against it. Basically, we figure everyone must be satisfied." The four-day school week is gaining acceptance in rural school districts, as administrators search for ways to cut budgets without cutting staff. Scattered districts in 13 states now operate on an abbreviated week, with the largest number in Colorado, said Paul Bauman, policy analyst for the Denver-based Education Commission of the States. In at least two other states, legislation has been introduced to permit four-day school weeks, he said. There have been no major studies analyzing the success of the four-day school week nationwide, said Bauman. A 1981 study of Colorado schools concluded that the system needed more time before it could be fairly evaluated, he said. Nationwide, the four-day week is limited to rural school districts, where many students spend their days off helping on the family ranch or farm, Bauman said. The grandfather of the four-day week is the 400-student Cimarron, N.M., school district, where a Tuesday-through-Friday schedule has been in effect for 10 years. Superintendent Joe Pompeo says that community would fire him if he switched back to a five-day week. In Oregon, Days Creek and Prospect, about 45 miles northeast of Medford, are winding up a one-year trial program approved by state school Superintendent Verne Duncan. Both districts want to keep the schedule and officials in Rogue River say they are considering a four-day week. Shifting to a shorter week required the Oregon school districts to get a one-year waiver from a state regulation that students spend 175 days a year in the classroom.

### Mixed-age grouping (early childhood)

Mixed-age grouping is an idea with a long history, so the available resources number in the thousands. We've limited our listings to recent resources for the age group with which it is most popular (young children in grades K-3, for the most part). Some of the things we've picked, however, do include a consideration of mixed-age grouping with older elementary children. Remember that the idea is widely applicable—adults certainly work in "mixed-age" groups; and in high schools, it's not uncommon for 9th grade students to take classes with 12th grade students. Also remember, "nongraded" means *mixed-aged,* not a change in student evaluation methods.

American Montessori Society Position Papers. (1994). *Montessori-Life,* 6(2), 6-7.

One of these position papers, "Mixed-age Grouping," describes eight methods and strategies for mixed-age practice that serve as guides for implementation.

Anderson, R. (1993). The return of the nongraded classroom. *Principal,* 72(3), 9-12.

This article makes a case that graded schools since the mid 1880s have promulgated lockstep curriculum; simplistic child development assumptions; and sexist, isolationist teaching methods. It says heterogeneous, mixed-age groupings in nongraded schools offer an alternative that takes about five years to launch.

Appalachia Educational Laboratory. (1993). *Notes from the field: Education reform in rural Kentucky, 3*(1-2), 1-17. (ERIC Document Reproduction Service No. ED 366 480; for previous volumes, see ED 360 120)

The two issues of this newsletter focus on reform efforts in four rural Kentucky school districts. The first issue describes Kentucky's ungraded primary program in eight elementary schools. It describes the six critical attributes that "full implementation" requires and assesses progress the schools made toward this goal. Observations reveal that six attributes are being implemented to some degree in most primary classrooms, but achieving "continuous progress" is difficult. The second issue in the volume deals with school-based decision making in the four school districts.

Appalachia Educational Laboratory. (1991). *Ungraded classrooms: Failsafe schools?* (Policy Brief). Charleston, WV: Author.

This short, readable publication defines terms, enumerates six essential ingredients of ungraded programs, provides pros and cons, and sets out what states can do to facilitate implementation of ungraded (mixed-age) programs. AEL will provide a master copy on white paper for reproduction on request. Call the Distribution Center at 800/624-9120, or write to AEL, P. O. Box 1348, Charleston, WV 25325-1348.

Davis, B., Frankovich, M., Chandler, V., Franklin, P., Nelson, D., Proffer, A., Valentine, L., Whittington, M., & Bennett, L. (1991). *Continuous progress with multi-age grouping and teacher teaming: A nongraded implementation guide for small school districts.* (ERIC Document Reproduction Service No. ED 337 341)

This is a guide for small school districts that want to use a mixed-age arrangement at the elementary school level (K-6). It recommends a 4-year phase-in for the arrangement, after which the authors advise that one additional grade can be brought into the multigrade system (through grade 6). It describes teaching teams, instruction, and evaluation related to the arrangement.

Fogarty, R. (Ed.). (1993). *The multiage classroom: A collection.* IRI/ Skylight Publishing. (ERIC Document Reproduction Service No. ED 369 574)

This collection of articles reviews literature on "mixed-age, nongraded, continuous progress" classrooms. The articles explore concerns, delineate procedures and practices, and illustrate classroom practice in 227 pages. Titles include "The Dual-Age Classroom: Questions and Answers"; "The Return of the Nongraded Classroom"; "The Pros and Cons of Mixed-age Grouping"; and "How I Learned to Stop Worrying and Love My Combination Class." Book available for $15.95 plus $5 shipping and handling from the publisher at 200 East Wood Street, Suite 274, Palatine, IL 60027. (Available only as a microfiche from the ERIC Document Reproduction Service; paper copy not available from EDRS.)

Gutierrez, R., & Slavin, R. (1992). Achievement effects of the nongraded elementary school: A best evidence synthesis. *Review of Educational Research, 62*(4), 333-76.

This article reviews research on how nongraded elementary school organization affects achievement. The authors say that positive impact can result if teachers are allowed to provide more direct instruction to students.

Katz, L. (1992). *Nongraded and mixed-age grouping in early childhood programs.* (ERIC Digest). Urbana, IL: ERIC Clearinghouse on Elementary and Early Childhood Education. (ERIC Document Reproduction Service No. ED 351 148)

This digest discusses terms related to mixed-age grouping that have important implications for teaching and curriculum. It defines "nongraded" (or "ungraded"), "combined classes," and "continuous progress," and relates these terms to the idea of mixed-age or multigrade grouping. These terms are used to emphasize the goal of using teaching practices that maximize the benefits of cooperation among children of various ages. Research indicates that, in spite of its risks, the potential advantages of mixed-age grouping outweigh its disadvantages.

Katz, L., Evangelou, D., & Hartman, J. (1990). *The case for mixed-age grouping in early education.* Urbana, IL, and Washington, DC: ERIC Clearinghouse on Elementary and Early Childhood Education and National Association for the Education of Young Children. (ERIC Document Reproduction Service No. ED 326 302)

In six brief chapters, mixed-age grouping of young children in schools and child care centers is explored and advocated. The book considers the advantages of mixed-age grouping, social and cognitive development, peer tutoring and cooperative learning, examples of successful programs, and four basic questions about implementing mixed-age grouping. A brief section that develops conclusions and recommendations concludes the book. It also contains a resource chapter with bibliography and suggestions for teachers working with mixed-age groups.

Kentucky Education Association and Appalachia Educational Laboratory. (1991). *Ungraded primary programs: Steps toward developmentally appropriate instruction.* Charleston, WV: Authors.

This study provides a rationale with effects, obstacles, and teaching strategies, along with 10 case studies and findings across programs. It includes an extensive bibliography and listing of resources with appendices; one is the ungraded primary program provisions of the Kentucky Education Reform Act. (Available from AEL, P. O. Box 1348, Charleston, WV 25325-1348; or call 800/624-9120.)

Miller, B. (1994). *Keeping children at the center: Implementing the multiage classroom.* Eugene, OR: ERIC Clearinghouse on Educational Management, University of Oregon. (ERIC/CEM Accession Number EA 025 954)

Defining multigrade classrooms as two or more grade levels intentionally placed together to improve learning, Miller describes commonalities of programs undertaken in four schools in the Northwest, including: innovative approaches to allow flexibility for children to learn at their own pace, communities of learners characterized by collegiality among teachers, cooperative learning, cross-age tutoring, and team teaching. Community volunteers became mainstays of instruction. Incremental steps that can facilitate change and improve the likelihood of success are identified and described. (Order from ERIC/CEM, 5207 University of Oregon, Eugene, OR 97403-5207, for $15.95 plus $3 shipping if paying by purchase order.)

Sumner, D. (Ed.). (1993). *Multiage classrooms: The upgrading of America's schools, the multiage resource book*. Peterborough, NH: Society for Developmental Education.

This book contains information on multigrade practice and instruction in mixed-age and mixed-grade-level classrooms through 24 reprinted articles, a 42-item bibliography, and profiles of 11 multigrade practice models. The final section of the book includes information and strategies for creation and implementation of multigrade programs. (Contact the Society for Developmental Education, Northgate, P. O. Box 577, Peterborough, NH 03458.)

University of Kentucky. (1994). *Kentucky's primary program: A progress report*. (1994). University of Kentucky Institute on Education Reform, Lexington, KY. (ERIC Document Reproduction Service No. ED 369 517)

This evaluation report documents progress that school districts have made toward implementing the Kentucky Education Reform Act of 1990 mandate that all elementary schools be nongraded, mixed-age, multiability primary schools by fall 1993. It notes that teachers have made some progress toward flexible physical environments, but classrooms are still teacher-dominated and have few learning centers or student-initiated activities. The report makes recommendations for staff development and school policy and provides copies of evaluation criteria, rating scales, and other instruments that evaluators used.

## Technology

There are thousands of articles, reports, and books about educational technology. Indeed, hundreds of such resources have been published in just the past two or three years. Our purpose here is to help you get started in exploring a field that may seem strange and confusing at first. The explosive growth of the World Wide Web and the new tools available for searching online information are making use of the Internet easier all the time.

The resources that follow are written for ordinary people and not for technological wizards. Topics include distance education, teleconferencing, and Internet resources. There are an amazing number of resources explaining the Internet that are available over the Internet itself (see the book by Kehoe, below, for example). We've also listed an article about technology (Hodas) that is available over the Internet.

We've included resources published no earlier than 1992—not only because of the volume of information available, but also because of the rapid pace of technological change. But there are lots of good ideas in the older literature, so do some digging. See the section at the end of this chapter that explains how to use ERIC, the national education information system.

This section is fairly comprehensive, and includes books, articles and reports about distance education and technology, articles and reports about telecommunications and electronic networking, and organizations.

**Books about technology.**

Barker, B. (1992). *The distance education handbook: An administrator's guide for rural and remote schools.* Charleston, WV: ERIC Clearinghouse on Rural Education and Small Schools. (ERIC Document Reproduction Service No. ED 340 547)

> This is one of the few handbooks on technology developed for a rural audience. It discusses options, purposes, costs, and the need for planning in simple terms. It describes 13 technologies in terms that anyone can understand. Available on ERIC microfiche only.

Kehoe, B. (1994). *Zen and the art of the Internet: A beginner's guide* (3rd Ed.). Englewood Cliffs, NJ: Prentice-Hall.

> This book is one of the first and most popular guides to the Internet. The first edition was distributed for free on the Internet and is still available at many anonymous ftp sites—for example, nic.merit.edu, directory introducing.the.internet, filename zen.txt. (Available from Simon & Schuster, 200 Old Tappan Road, Old Tappan, NJ 07675; 800/922-0579 [$23.95].)

LaQuey, T. (1993). *The Internet companion plus: A beginner's start-up kit for global networking.* Reading, MA: Addison-Wesley.

> This is a good guide for the true beginner, useful even for the pre-beginner who has not yet signed on to the Internet. (Available from Addison-Wesley, Route 128, Redding, MA 01867; 800/447-2226 [$19.95; includes diskette].)

Postman, N. (1992). *Technopoly: The surrender of culture to technology.* New York: Knopf.

This book is very different from any of the other resources listed here. The author suggests that technology is monopolizing our lives. It discusses big ideas in simple language. Rural people, especially, need to understand the downside of technology, so they have a better chance at minimizing the risks and maximizing the advantages of using technology. (Available from Alfred A. Knopf, Inc., 400 Hahn Road, Westminster, MD 21157; 800/733-3000 [$11.00, paperback].)

Tennant, R., Ober, J., & Lipow, A. (1993). *Crossing the Internet threshold: An instructional handbook.* Berkeley, CA: Library Solutions Press.

Like Kehoe and LaQuey, this handbook explains how to use the Internet. A unique feature is that it includes training materials to help others learn to use Internet resources. (Available from Library Solutions Press, 1100 Industrial Road, Suite 9, San Carols, CA 94070 [$45.00 with diskette, $35.00 without].)

**Articles and reports about technology** (distance education and technology planning).

Barker, B., & Taylor, D. (1993, July). *An overview of distance learning and telecommunications in rural schools.* Paper presented at the annual conference of the National Association of Counties, Chicago, IL. (ERIC Document Reproduction Service No. ED 365 502)

One of the more recent overviews of this topic, the paper distinguishes between classroom-focused options (distance education) and network-focused options (the Internet, commercial networks, and bulletin board systems).

Charron, E., & Obbink, K. (1993). Long-distance learning. *Science Teacher, 60*(3), 56-60.

This article considers key issues to weigh when choosing distance education courses, including communication with instructor and students, hands-on learning opportunities, equipment needed, accessibility of technical assistance, and intended audiences of courses offered.

Hodas, S. (1993). Technology refusal and the organizational culture of schools. *Educational Policy Analysis Archives* [On-line serial], *1*(10). Available e-mail: listserv@asuacad.bitnet Message: GET HODAS V1N10 F=MAIL.

This article links the failure of technology in schools to a clash between the values inherent in technology and those in the school organization, rather than to poor planning or implementation. (Also available as an ERIC document, ERIC Document Reproduction Service No. ED 366 328.)

Morgan, W. (1994). The cost of connecting: Distance learning can be affordable. *School Business Affairs, 60*(1), 50-53.

The author reviews some of the fundamentals of distance education systems and develops a cost-analysis model for introducing telecourses.

Ross, T., & Stewart, G. (1993). Facility planning for technology implementation. *Educational Facility Planner, 31*(3), 9-12.

This article describes features of facility planning relevant to technology—space, electricity, lighting, security, furnishings, shielding, and acoustics.

Schiller, S. (1993). Multimedia equipment for distance education. *Media and Methods, 30*(2), 36-37.

Describing basic multimedia equipment for distance education, this article includes general information on cable television, fiber optics, and interactive television and satellite technology.

Stammen, R. (1992). Computer conferencing: Perspectives of rural school administrators. *Rural Educator, 13*(2), 24-27.

This article considers rural school administrators' concerns. The author found computer conferencing use was minimal, but interest high.

Wagner, E. (1993). *A technology primer for distance educators.* Boulder, CO: Western Interstate Commission for Higher Education, Cooperative for Educational Communications. (ERIC Document Reproduction Service No. ED 366 313)

This book describes technical information in straightforward terms, including transport mechanics, network facilities, audioconferences, audiographic teleconferences, computer conferences, video teleconferences, and both narrow-band and broadband interactive distance learning technologies.

**Articles and reports about technology** (networking and telecommunications).

Burleigh, M., & Weeg, P. (1993). KIDLINK: A challenging and safe place for children across the world. *Information Development, 9*(3), 147-157.

KIDLINK uses the Internet and other networks to connect kids 10 to 15 years old all around the world. It includes a list of contact points in 29 nations.

Descy, D. (1993). Where to start: An Internet resource guide. *TechTrends, 38*(5), 39-40.

The guide overviews beginners' resources and includes works on introductory materials, technical manuals, and a guide especially for elementary and secondary school teachers. Three new services on the Internet are also described.

Eisenberg, M. (1992). *Networking K-12* (ERIC Digest). Syracuse, NY: ERIC Clearinghouse on Information and Technology. (ERIC Document Reproduction Service No. ED 354 903)

This four-page report reviews the relevance of computer networking (the Internet and similar services) to instruction in elementary and secondary schools. An overview is provided to use with groups. (Call the ERIC Clearinghouse on Information and Technology, 800/464-9107 to request a free copy. Also available from the AskERIC Virtual Library [gopher to ericir.syr.edu].)

Giguere, M. (1993). The Internet: A selective annotated bibliography of print material. *Education Libraries, 17*(2), 13-20.

This bibliography overviews a variety of resources about the Internet for novices to consult *before* getting involved. It lists 38 print sources and includes materials about such Internet applications as electronic mail, remote login, and file transfer; and information about Internet tools such as Archie, Gopher, and WAIS (Wide Area Information Server).

Honey, M., & Henriquez, A. (1993). *Telecommunications and K-12 educators: Findings from a national survey.* New York: Center for Technology in Education. (ERIC Document Reproduction Service No. ED 359 923)

This book is one of the few systematic national surveys of Internet use among teachers in elementary and high schools. It describes the extent of use for various purposes and activities, barriers to use, and includes recommendations for improving usage. Also included is an extensive list of service providers.

Hughes, D. (1993). Appropriate and distributed networks: A model for K-12 educational telecommunications. *Internet Research, 3*(4), 22-29.

The article describes a model for networking where local computer bulletin boards at the school level connect with the Internet. Issues considered include communications software, graphics, training and administrative support, public readiness, and cost estimates.

Raish, M. (1993). *Network knowledge for the neophyte: Stuff you need to know in order to navigate the electronic village* (Version 3.0). (ERIC Document Reproduction Service No. ED 360 961)

This guide is available from both ERIC and via Internet "File Transfer Protocol" (FTP) at the Internet address given. Like other resources given, it discusses basic Internet functions. In addition to ERIC, this resource is also available over the Internet via FTP: hydra.uwo.ca Directory pub/libsoft File: NETWORK_KNOWLEDGE_for_the_NEOPH.TXT.

Tuss, J. (1994). Roadmaps to the Internet: Finding the best guidebook for your needs. *Online, 18*(1), 14-16, 18-22, 25-26.

The author reviews and compares 11 books about the Internet, including four that concentrate on how to get connected, one for teaching about the Internet, five that are guides to using the Internet, and one that examines how special librarians are using the Internet. A sidebar lists 18 additional titles.

**Organizations involved in technology.**

Consortium for School Networking (CoSN)
P. O. Box 6519
Washington, DC  20035-5193
voice:  202/466-6296
e-mail:  cosn@bitnic.bitnet
gopher: cosn.org

> The Consortium takes action, especially at the national level, to promote widespread access for K-12 schools to on-line resources. CoSN operates a gopher site and an electronic discussion group. Memberships are by fee; different rates apply to individuals, schools, and school districts.

ERIC Clearinghouse on Information and Technology (ERIC/IT)
Syracuse University
Center for Science and Technology
4th Floor, Room 194
Syracuse, NY  13244-4100
voice:  800/464-9107
e-mail:  askeric@ericir.syr.edu
gopher: ericir.syr.edu

> ERIC/IT is the ERIC clearinghouse that specializes in libraries, instructional media, and technology.  It abstracts the major educational journals, as well as relevant documents and books, and produces a variety of useful publications.

> The AskERIC Virtual Library is located at ERIC/IT.  To use the library, gopher to ericir.syr.edu.  A great deal of information about educational technology can be accessed via the AskERIC Virtual Library.  For more information about ERIC and its services, consult the section of this chapter devoted to ERIC.

National Center for Technology Planning
Larry S. Anderson, director
Drawer NU
Mississippi State, MS  39762
voice phone:  601/325-2281
e-mail:  LSA1@Ra.MsState.edu

The Center collects technology plans, disseminates information about technology planning, and provides technical assistance to educators and others. The plans collected by the Center are available in fulltext electronic form, via the Internet.

## Pulling Together—A Wealth of Other Options

*Pulling Together: R&D Resources for Rural Schools* is a publication of the 10 regional educational laboratories. Regional labs serve states and territories in a given region, where their major efforts are devoted to research and development projects directed at school improvement. Beginning in 1987, each laboratory began to focus a portion of its resources on developing useful publications, model programs, services, and training programs for rural educators and others concerned with rural education (including parents and community members). The laboratories have, over the years, also developed many other resources (many described in the ERIC database) that may be useful in rural settings. You may want to confer with representatives of rural programs at the lab serving your region (a list of the labs concludes this entry).

*Pulling Together* describes the results of the labs' decade-long effort to create resources especially for rural schools and communities. It is organized around six themes identified as important by rural scholars:

- rural school effectiveness,
- curricular provisions,
- school and community partnerships,
- human resources,
- technological resources, and
- governance and finance.

These themes relate to many of the issues considered in this handbook. The bulk of *Pulling Together* is six chapters that describe resources—over 250 of them—developed specifically with rural schools and communities in mind. Resources are coded as publications, model programs, services, or training programs. The text provides complete availability and contact information for listed resources. Some materials have been developed specifically with the rural parts of the region served by a particular laboratory in mind. Other materials have in mind a national audience of rural educators and community members.

*Pulling Together* is available from:

Appalachia Educational Laboratory (AEL)
The Rural Center
P. O. Box 1348
Charleston, WV  25325
Contact:  Hobart Harmon
800/624-9120
fax: 304/347-0487
e-mail: harmonh@ael.org  or  howleyc@ael.org
Serves Appalachia Region: KY, TN, VA, WV

WestEd Headquarters (formerly Far West Laboratory for Educational
Research and Development)
Rural Education
730 Harrison St.
San Francisco, CA  94107-1242
Contact:  Tom Ross
415/565-3000
fax: 415/565-3012
e-mail: tross@fwl.org
Serves Western Region: AZ, CA, NV, UT

Mid-Atlantic Laboratory for Student Success (LSS)
Temple University
Center for Research in Human Development and Education
933 Ritter Annex
13th St. & Cecil B. Moore
Philadelphia, PA  19122
Contact:  Margaret C. Wang, Executive Director
215/204-3030
fax: 215/204-5130
e-mail: mcw@vm.temple.edu
States served:  DC, DE, MD, NJ, PA

Mid-Continent Regional Educational Laboratory (McREL)
Rural Education Program
2550 South Parker Rd., Ste 500
Aurora, CO  80014
Contact:  Richard Rangel
303/743-5572
303/337-0990
fax: 303/337-3005
Serves Central Region:  CO, KS, MO, NE, ND, SD, WY

North Central Regional Educational Laboratory (NCREL)
Rural Initiatives
1900 Spring Rd., Ste 300
Oak Brook, IL 60521-1480
Contact: Joseph D'Amico
708/571-4700
fax: 708/571-4716
Serves Midwestern Region: IA, IL, IN, MI, MN, OH, WI

Northeast and Islands Laboratory at Brown University (LAB)
164 Angell St., Box 1929
Providence, RI 02912
Contact: Adeline Becker, Executive Director
401/863-2770
fax: 401/421-7650
e-mail: adeline_becker@brown.edu
Serves Northeastern Region: CT, MA, ME, NH, NY, PR, RI, VI, VT

Northwest Regional Educational Laboratory (NWREL)
Rural Education Program
101 SW Main St., Ste 500
Portland, OR 97204
Contact: Steve Nelson
503/275-9500 or 800/547-6339
fax: 503/275-9489
e-mail: ruraled@nwrel.org
Serves Northwestern Region: AK, ID, MT, OR, WA

Pacific Region Educational Laboratory (PREL)
828 Fort St. Mall, Ste 500
Honolulu, HI 96813
Contact: John Kofel, Executive Director
808/533-6000
fax: 808/533-7599
Serves Pacific Region: American Samoa, Commonwealth of the Northern
Mariana Islands, Federated States of Micronesia, Guam, Hawaii, Republic
of the Marshall Islands, Republic of Palau

SouthEastern Regional Vision for Education (SERVE)
P.O. Box 5367
Greensboro, NC 27435
Contact: Gina Burkhardt
919/334-3211 or 800/755-3277
fax: 919/334-3268
Serves Southeastern Region: AL, FL, GA, MS, NC, SC

Southwest Educational Development Laboratory (SEDL)
Rural Small Schools Initiative
211 E Seventh St.
Austin, TX 78701-3281
Contact: Deborah V. Jolly
512/476-6861
fax: 512/476-2286
Serves Southwestern Region: AR, LA, NM, OK, TX

## Tools for Finding Information

Under the headings "Coalition Building/Getting Organized" and "Needs Assessment," we considered local sources of information. This section considers other sources—organizations and establishments that are officially in the information business.

In the United States, there are an almost unbelievable number of these organizations. The ones listed are among the most helpful to people interested in rural and small schools. Our aim here is to let you know the basics about a variety of organizations whose job it is to get information into the hands of the public. Knowledge about these organizations is less common than you'd expect. But they are all very easy to reach. The entries are divided into the following categories:

• ERIC (the Educational Resources Information Center and its 16 clearinghouses); and

• Libraries, OPACs (Internet-Accessible Online Library Catalogs, including the Library of Congress), and CD-ROMs.

These resources make available a great deal of information that usually is hard to get in small, rural communities. But a little effort will bring you exactly the same information that is available to people in urban areas and to professionals. Moreover, many resources can be accessed via telephone, some through toll-free numbers.

Some of this information is available electronically. And in many rural communities (not all!), there are some people who are connected to electronic information services. For this reason, the section that follows includes e-mail numbers and other electronic details where relevant.

**ERIC in a nutshell.** The Educational Resources Information Center (ERIC) is a federally funded, nationwide network designed to give the public ready access to information about education. A comprehensive booklet that explains ERIC is available free from ACCESS ERIC (800/LET-ERIC). Ask for a copy of *All About ERIC*.

- At the heart of ERIC is the largest education database in the world—containing more than 800,000 records.

- The ERIC records describe journal articles, research reports, curriculum and teaching guides, conference papers, and books. Each year approximately 30,000 new records are added.

- Items described in ERIC records can be ordered over the telephone. Some are already available in fulltext forms via electronic media. ERIC services, moreover, are available at thousands of locations nationwide.

ERIC presents education information in a format convenient to users. More than 20 years ago, ERIC became the first commercial online database. In 1986, the ERIC database became available for searching on CD-ROM (compact disk, read-only memory). Now, via the Internet, ERIC information is accessible to millions of people from their offices and homes, all over the world.

**Key units in the ERIC network.** The ERIC network includes these units, all of which can be reached via toll-free telephone numbers and electronic mail, in addition to regular surface mail:

- 16 clearinghouses (each of which specializes in different sections of the educational literature);

- ACCESS ERIC (a first stop for general information about education or about the ERIC network; 800/LET-ERIC); and

- the ERIC Document Reproduction Service (EDRS), which produces and sells microfiche and paper copies of ERIC documents; 800/443-ERIC.

**Some important details about ERIC.** All of the units described above—clearinghouses, ACCESS ERIC, and EDRS—provide products and services to anyone who contacts them, either for free or for comparatively low cost.

It's important to realize that the ERIC database—with its more than 800,000 records—is divided into two parts—*one part for journal articles* and *one part for everything else.* Let's take "everything else" first.

* "Everything else" (besides articles) is called *Resources in Education* (RIE); it's ERIC's original project, begun in the mid 1960s.

   — The RIE not only describes items, but it is associated most of the time (via an "ERIC Document Number") with a miniaturized photographic image of the document, called a "microfiche." Paper copies can be made from the microfiche.

   — Copies of ERIC documents (those with ED numbers, for example, "ED 312 115") are usually available from the ERIC Document Reproduction Service (EDRS). So if you find an ED item you want, you can get it rather easily by calling EDRS at 800/443-ERIC. To place a phone order, all you need is the ED number and a credit card.

* Journal articles (and *only* journal articles) are described in *The Current Index to Journals in Education (CIJE)*, begun in 1969, as the idea of ERIC began to catch on, and as users began to expect ERIC to cover the journal literature.

   — Instead of "ED numbers," records about ERIC journal articles are assigned an "EJ" number.

   — ERIC does not make microfiches of EJ items. Instead, article reprint vendors, through no connection with ERIC, make copies of journal articles from all fields (not just education) available to the public.

   — Two major article reprint vendors are University Microfilms International, 800/521-0600, ext. 2786; and Institute for Scientific Information, 800/523-1850.

**The importance of going to the library.** Most libraries also have print copies of the *CIJE* and the *RIE*, and most also have the ERIC database on CD-ROM. For doing some serious digging, a trip to a college or university library can be amazingly useful. ACCESS ERIC can help you locate the best and nearest academic library for this purpose.

College and university libraries often maintain an ERIC microfiche collection. They also subscribe to a variety of education journals, according to the needs of the training programs they offer to teachers and school administrators. If you have a number of items—EJ items or ED items—you want to get copies of to take home and read, go to an academic library.

**Playing the system: Other alternatives.** If you can't go to the library or if you don't have the time to learn how to search the ERIC database, ERIC is still one of the most useful information networks around. Some

ERIC clearinghouses will do free database searches for people. One of these is the ERIC Clearinghouse on Rural Education and Small Schools, located in Charleston, West Virginia:

ERIC Clearinghouse on Rural Education and Small Schools
P. O. Box 1348
Charleston, WV  25328-1348
voice: 800/624-9120
e-mail: lanhamb@ael.org
WWW: http://www.ael.org

With the results of your database search in hand, you can call EDRS for copies of ERIC documents:

ERIC Document Reproduction Service
7420 Fullerton Road, Suite 110
Springfield, VA  22153-2852
voice: 800/443-3742
e-mail: edrs@inet.ed.gov
WWW: http://edrs.com

For copies of ERIC journal articles, you can get in touch with several organizations that will supply your needs. Contact information for these organizations follows. Please note that the first organization (CARL UnCover) provides services *only* via the Internet and as of this writing covers only the years 1988 and later. UMI and ISI take orders by mail and phone, and they include articles published before 1988.

Colorado Alliance of Research Libraries
CARL UnCover (electronic search and ordering service)
e-mail: help@carl.org
telnet: pac.carl.org

UMI InfoStore
500 Sansome St., Ste 44
San Francisco, CA  94111
voice: 800/248-0360
e-mail: achorder@umi.com

Institute for Scientific Information (ISI)
Genuine Article Service
3501 Market Street
Philadelphia, PA  19104
voice: 800/523-1850
e-mail: tga@isinet.com

For basic information about ERIC and its varied services, you'll want to speak with someone at ACCESS ERIC, the ERIC unit whose mission is to help enhance public use of ERIC. ACCESS ERIC publishes a journal free to the public (*The ERIC Review*). They can also send you a free copy of *All About ERIC*, a handy guide to the ERIC network—including telephone numbers, e-mail addresses, and tips on searching the ERIC database.

ACCESS ERIC
1600 Research Boulevard, 5F
Rockville, MD 20850-3172
voice: 800/LET-ERIC (800/538-3742)
e-mail: acceric@inet.ed.gov
WWW: http://www.aspensys.com/eric/

If you have an Internet account, your access to ERIC can be more immediate. You can ask a question by e-mail or you can connect to the AskERIC Virtual Library.

* First, you can put any question (related to education) to an ERIC staff member by writing to askeric@ericir.syr.edu. Be specific in your question. Let ERIC know: (1) what sorts of documents interest you most (for instance, literature reviews, research studies, program descriptions, instructional materials); (2) what grade levels interest you, generally (for instance, primary, elementary, middle school, high school); and (3) something about your situation—why this question is important to you. If you take time to do this, you'll get a better answer than you would otherwise.

* Second, you can reach the AskERIC Virtual Library (a "gopher" site) by gophering to ericir.syr.edu. If your Internet provider doesn't offer gopher service, you can still reach the AskERIC gopher site by telnetting to ericir.syr.edu. Once connected, access the National Gopher System, and move through the following directories:

Other Gopher and Information Servers/
   North America/
      USA/
         General/
            AskERIC - (Educational Resources
            Information Center)

The ERIC network is fundamental to your efforts to get up-to-date information about education, but there are many other tools that are very important. Descriptions of a few of these tools are considered briefly under the headings that follow.

**Libraries.** ERIC works with libraries as one route to get its materials to the public. And, as noted above, going to the library can be very helpful. Not only do libraries house ERIC microfiche collections and maintain journal collections, but they house books. Indeed, the very word "library" comes from a Latin word meaning "book."

There are a lot of books on education. Many cannot be found in your local public library so, again, libraries at colleges and universities are a good source of information. If you know what books you'd like to get, however, you should investigate the procedures for "interlibrary loan" at your nearest public library. Not every library can buy every book that anyone might want, and loans between libraries are increasingly common.

The trouble is, how do you find out what books you need to read? In school most of us were advised to "use the card catalog." But if your local library has just a few books on schools and education, this advice won't be much help.

**OPACs.** The trouble is finding the *right* card catalog—the one that indexes the most books. This is where *Online Public Access Catalogs* (or "OPACs" as they are known in electronic media) come in.

OPACs have emerged over the past 15 years or so as libraries have computerized their card catalogs. With everything in electronic format, and with computer networks making e-mail and file transfers and other things possible, libraries began to go public with their computerized card catalogs.

That's the basic idea—OPACs are computerized card catalogs that you can access from wherever you have an electronic network connection (either through some form of Internet access or through a direct dialup connection via a modem).

So where's the biggest electronic card catalog? The Library of Congress, of course. But there are thousands of others, and they're not located in just the United States. OPACs are coming online all over the world. You can, at this writing, search the OPACs of libraries in London, Budapest, Stockholm, and Tokyo.

To connect to the Library of Congress OPAC, you must first connect to the Internet. You can connect to the OPAC using either gopher or telnet:

gopher: marvel.loc.gov
telnet: locis.loc.gov

LOCIS requires some experience to use well, but LOCIS searching manuals are available online and in a printed version from the Library's Cataloging Distribution Service at 202/707-6100.

**OPAC guides.** There are, as we noted, thousands of OPACs. One commercially published, printed reference guide is:

Rega, R. (1993). *OPAC directory 1993: An annual guide to online public access catalogs and databases.* Westport, CT: Meckler.

Printed OPAC guides like this are probably most useful to those without Internet connection. Even if you don't have Internet access, you can still dial directly into many OPACs. That is, you can have your modem dial in directly to the OPAC, without going through the Internet. This particular directory provides details about modem settings and login procedures. (Available from Meckler Corporation, 11 Ferry Lane, W., Westport, CT 068880; 203/226-6967.)

But printed guides are largely unnecessary to Internet users, because most Internet service providers offer a range of options that makes connecting to OPACs very easy.

**Useful reference works about education in the United States.** There are many reference works in education. We've selected those that we think would be most helpful to people concerned with rural and small schools. Some are very general, some relate directly to rural education, and some can help you put rural education in a larger context. We've also included a couple of very useful electronic products (two CD-ROM products and a diskette product).

## Books

Hammer, P. (comp.). (1996). *Rural education directory: Organizations and resources.* Charleston, WV: ERIC Clearinghouse on Rural Education and Small Schools.

National Diffusion Network. (1994). *Educational programs that work: The catalogue of the National Diffusion Network (NDN)* (20th ed.). Sopris West: Longmont, CO. [Available for $13.95 plus S&H, from the publisher at 1140 Boston Avenue, Longmont, CO 80501; 800/547-6747; for previous editions in the ERIC database, see ED 338 616, ED 338 617, ED 338 618, ED 370 939.]

Smith, T., Rogers, G., Alsalam, N., Perie, M., Mahoney, R., & Martin, V. (1994). *The condition of education, 1994.* Washington, DC: National Center for Education Statistics, U. S. Department of Education. [Available from the Government Printing Office, Superintendent of Documents, P. O. Box 371954, Pittsburgh, PA 15250-7954; call the order desk at 202/512-1800 for information about the most current edition of this annually produced report.]

Stern, J. (Ed.) (1994). *The condition of education in rural schools.* Washington, DC: Office of Educational Research and Improvement, U. S. Department of Education. (ERIC Document Reproduction Service No. ED 371 935)

## CD-ROM Products (three noted)

1. The entire ERIC database describing over 850,000 resources (from ERIC's *Resources in Education* and *Current Index to Journals in Education*) is available on a very low-cost CD-ROM product from the National Information Services Company (NISC).

   features: subscription price: $100.00 (for individuals)
   contents: both RIE and CIJE, 1966-present
   2 disks (archival, 1966/1979; current 1980-present)
   updates: quarterly
   includes *ERIC Thesaurus* on disk
   operating system: DOS (IBM-compatible)
   other: Spanish-language user interface available

   available from: ERIC Processing and Reference Facility
   1301 Piccard Drive, Suite 300
   Rockville, MD 20850-4305
   toll-free: 800/799-3742
   fax: 301/258-5500
   Internet: ericfac@inet.ed.gov

2. The Oryx Press produces another low-cost ERIC CD-ROM product. This one contains descriptions of education-related journal articles described in ERIC's *Current Index to Journals in Education* only (that is, it excludes approximately 400,000 resources archived on ERIC microfiche as *Resources in Education*). This product is contained on a single CD-ROM rather than multiple disks.

   features: subscription price: $99.00 (for individuals)
   CIJE only, 1969-present
   1 disk
   updates: quarterly
   includes *ERIC Thesaurus* on disk
   operating system: DOS or Windows (IBM-compatibles)
   other features: relevancy ranking of found articles

   available from: Oryx Press
   4041 North Central Avenue at Indian School
   Suite 700
   Phoenix, AZ 85012-3397
   toll-free: 800/279-6799
   fax: 800/279-4663
   Internet: info@oryxpress.com

3.  The National Center for Education Statistics produces a CD-ROM product called EDSearch (education statistics on disk). It presents statistical data in a wealth of figures and tables (1,800 all told) from major NCES statistical reports, including the *Digest of Education Statistics*, the *Condition of Education*, *Projections of Education Statistics*, *Youth Indicators*, and *Historical Trends*. For more information about *EDSearch*, please contact:

National Center for Education Statistics
Education Information Office
800/424-1616

Ask for information about *EDSearch* (NCES No. 94670) or the latest update (released annually, generally in October).

# INDEX

Courts, 95-96, 97
Criticism: of rural schools, 5, 28
CSSO. See Chief state school officer
Curriculum development, 31, 32; resources on, 40-41.
    See also Course offerings

de Tocqueville, Alexis, 9
Decision making, 100; administrators and, 91, 97; chief state
    school officers and, 95; courts and, 96; teachers and, 92
Dewey, John, 48
DeYoung, Alan, 41
Disadvantaged students, 31
Distance education, 78, 81; resources on, 134-36

Economic conditions, 4, 28
Economic development: rural schools and, 55; schooling and,
    52-61; strategies, 60
Economies of scale, 22, 32-36. See also School finance
Economy, 18; core sector of, 55; peripheral sector of, 55;
    rural, 54-55, 59-61
Education Commission of the States, 90
Education reform, 32; history of, 15-25. See also School reform
Educational research. See Research studies; Resources
Educational Resources Information Center. See ERIC
Educational role groups, 89-101
Educational technology. See Technology
Effective schools movement, 91
Efficiency, 20, 32, 35
Electronic mail, 77, 81. See also Technology
Employers: urban versus rural, 8
Employment: and technology, 72-75
Energy conservation, 59
Enrollment, 4; curriculum and, 28-29; in public versus
    private schools, 20-21
ERIC, 88-89, 138, 143-47
Experiential education: resources on, 122-23

Factory model of schooling, 16-17, 19, 58-59, 63, 68, 70, 71, 73
Faculty senates, 92
Families. See Parents
FFA. See Future Farmers of America
Four-day school week, 2, 63-67, 73-74, 97; resources on, 125-28